Linda's Kitchen

Linda's Kitchen

SIMPLE AND INSPIRING RECIPES FOR MEATLESS MEALS

LINDA McCARTNEY

Food Consultant
Rosamond Richardson

Photography
Debbie Patterson

A Bulfinch Press Book
Little, Brown and Company
Boston New York Toronto London

To my family and all veggies,
present and future

Like all diets, a vegetarian diet should be a balanced one.
If you have any doubts or concern about whether your diet is suitable
you should consult your doctor. Additionally, if you have allergies
you should not use those recipes that contain ingredients to which you
may be allergic or otherwise affected.

Introduction copyright © 1995 by MPL Communications Ltd
Text and photographs copyright © 1995 by
Little, Brown and Company (Inc.)

First Edition

ISBN 0-8212-2123-X

Library of Congress Catalog Card Number 95–75416
A CIP catalogue for this book is available
from the British Library

Food styling: Jane Suthering
Designer: Janet James

Published simultaneously in the United States of America
by Bulfinch Press, an imprint and trademark of
Little, Brown and Company (Inc.),
in Great Britain by Little, Brown and Company (UK),
and in Canada by Little, Brown & Company (Canada) Limited

PRINTED AND BOUND IN GERMANY

The author would like to thank Paul, Heather, Mary, Stella,
James, Louise, Robby and team, Viv and team, Carol Judy and team,
Geoff, Pat, Sherrie, Marie, Sue, Shelagh, Louise, Laura,
Monique, Ann, Mike, Ian, Tim and team, John, Sharon, and everyone
who helped and shared a veggie recipe.

The publishers would like to thank Laura Ashley for permission
to reproduce the fabric used on the cover (Glenisla Check
in cowslip; for further information call 01628 770345) and Ian Mankin
for permission to reproduce that used in the menu planners
(Carlton Plaid in mustard; for further information call 0171 371 8825).

The photograph on page one features edible flower garnishes
(see page 147)

CONTENTS

Ⓥ INDICATES A VEGAN DISH

Introduction

When my husband asked me why I was writing another cookbook, it made me realize how time had flown – and how far vegetarian cuisine had progressed in the intervening years. When I wrote my first cookbook, it was to show my family and friends how easy it was to become a vegetarian. But now our eating habits have changed, most of us are trying to cut down on fatty foods, and I felt the time had come to bring things up to date and to increase the range of easily prepared recipes that are available to today's cook.

Even if you find cooking daunting, I hope to bring out the creative cook in you. It may be that you've always thought of vegetarian meals as tiresome to prepare and bland in taste – in which case there's a surprise in store for you. Vegetarian cooking is easy, it's tasty, and it's good for your body, too. Recent research has shown that a vegetarian diet can dramatically lessen the risk of – among other things – heart disease, angina, cancer, diabetes, and high blood pressure.

Some people believe that they are vegetarian if they just cut out red meat, but a vegetarian eats no meat, and no fish either. If you go veggie, it means no animal dies for your plate. I've met a lot of people who say, "I'm almost veggie, but I still eat fish." To me that's like being "almost pregnant" – either you are or you aren't. I know that for some people cutting out fish is the most difficult obstacle on the road to vegetarianism. But fish have feelings too, and anyone who has ever seen a fish hooked out of the water, jerking and gasping for breath, should realize that. The "bountiful sea" does *not* exist for us to plunder at will, and perhaps if we started thinking in terms of sea*life* instead of sea*food* our appetite for fish might be lost.

Of course tradition is responsible for much of today's meaty diet. For most of us in the West, meat and two veg is a standard meal and, for many people, Sundays are not complete without a roast meat dinner. But the world has changed since those traditions developed. Many more people share this planet and, as the population grows, it is simply not going to be possible to feed everyone on a meat-based diet. There just isn't enough grazing land for all the livestock required.

For me, that's a good enough reason in itself for becoming a vegetarian – because if we fed the starving people of the world the grain we use to fatten farm animals there really could be enough to go around. If everyone in the West reduced their meat consumption by just ten percent, it would free up enough grazing land to grow food for up to 40 million people. So, being a vegetarian is not only better for you, it's better for everyone.

There are other lives that will be saved if you go veggie – the lives of the millions of animals that are slaughtered every year. Butchered in such horrific ways that if slaughterhouses had glass walls, we'd all be vegetarian. So, be a life-saver and a world-saver, and start a whole new way of life.

There are meals for all to enjoy here – from vegan meals to meals for the truck driver who reckons he'd miss his meat (…but he won't), to kids' meals, low-calorie meals, meals for entertaining, and family meals including a vegetarian Sunday lunch. While you're cooking, don't be afraid to adapt these recipes to suit yourself. I've tried to make taste the main ingredient in all of them; so get into the kitchen, rattle those pots and pans, have fun, and save lives while you're doing it – yours, the animals', and the planet's.

Linda McCartney

MENU PLANNER

A Dinner Party for 8

CHEESE PALMIERS 48

AVOCADO, MOZZARELLA AND TOMATO SALAD (x2) 134

SPAGHETTINI WITH SUN-DRIED TOMATOES, EGGPLANT AND CHILI (x2) 90

SPECIAL ARUGULA SALAD WITH SPINACH AND PARMESAN (x2) 129

LEMON SOUFFLÉ TART 167

A Family Lunch for 4 ♥

ASPARAGUS SOUP 25

CRISPY MUSHROOM LAYERS 71

WATERCRESS SALAD WITH GARLIC CROUTONS 136

FRUIT SORBET 160

A Supper for 4

ZUCCHINI AND WATERCRESS SOUP 26

EGGPLANT AND HERB CASSEROLE (halved) 66

GARLIC MASHED POTATOES 106

LEMON GREEN BEANS 44

An Easter Menu for 10

ASPARAGUS WITH GARLIC (x3) 44

OR WITH HOLLANDAISE (x2) 150

CREAMY VEGETABLE PIE (x2) 112

NOODLE BAKE (x2) 60

SAUTÉ OF SWEET POTATOES (x4) 105

SHREDDED ZUCCHINI SALAD (x2) 141

REDCURRANT CHEESECAKE 166

MOUSSE MADE WITH LEMONS 160

FOR SPRING

A Light Buffet
for 20

PARTY EGGS (x3) 49

CRISP FILO MUSHROOM
PARCELS 50

FILO CHEESE STRAWS
(x2) 48

CHEESE AND NUT
PÂTÉ (x2) 47

STUFFED BELL PEPPERS
(x3) 68

CHEESE AND BROCCOLI
QUICHE (x2) 115

SPICY RAW MUSHROOM
SALAD (x2) 136

CAESAR SALAD (x2) 133

TECHNICOLOR BEAN
SALAD 142

PECAN PIE (x2) 166

CHEESECAKE MADE WITH
BLACK CURRANTS 166

A French Menu
for 4

WARM GOAT CHEESE
SALAD 133

VEGETABLE
MILLE-FEUILLES WITH
PESTO 116

SCALLOPED POTATOES 107

PROVENÇAL PEPPER
SALAD 139

CRÈME BRÛLÉE 163

A Chinese Menu
for 6

VEGETABLE SPRING
ROLLS 110

STIR-FRY OF SPRING
VEGETABLES WITH
NOODLES (x1½) 56

RICE NOODLES WITH
BROCCOLI, GINGER AND
GARLIC 93

CHINESE EGG FRIED RICE 94

SWEET AND SOUR SAUCE 153

MANGO SORBET 160

A Birthday Party
for 4

CRISP FILO MUSHROOM
PARCELS 50

GOAT CHEESE AND
DILL SOUFFLÉ 82

PASTA TWISTS WITH
SPINACH AND NUTS 88

CAESAR SALAD 133

CHOCOLATE SPONGE
WITH CHOCOLATE BUTTER
FROSTING 175
DECORATED WITH
CANDLES AND FLOWERS

MENU PLANNER

A Teenagers' Party for 15

PARTY EGGS (x1½) 49
FILO CHEESE STRAWS (x2) 48
MEXICAN CORN BREAD (x2) 34
NACHOS (x2) 33
EASY PIZZA 117
TASTY BEANBURGERS (x4) 55
LIGHT SAUSAGE ROLLS (x2) 49
CRISPY POTATO SKINS (x2) 105
CARROT SALAD 134
SOUR CREAM ONION DIP 156 WITH TORTILLA CHIPS

CHOCOLATE CHIP COOKIES 176
BAKED CHOCOLATE PUDDING WITH FUDGE SAUCE (x2) 162
CARROT CAKE 172

A Barbecue for 12

DILL CUCUMBER DIP (x2) 156 WITH CRUDITÉS
SOUR CREAM ONION DIP 156

MARINATED VEGETARIAN SAUSAGES AND BURGERS (x2) 119
CRUSTY GARLIC POTATOES (x2) 125
VEGETABLE KEBABS (x2) 119
CHAR-GRILLED MUSHROOMS WITH ROSEMARY AND GARLIC (x2) 120
ZUCCHINI WITH HERBS (x2) 124
MEXICAN CORN BREAD (x2) 34
BARBECUE SAUCE 153
SALSAS 152
ROASTED RED PEPPER SAUCE 149
TARRAGON AND MUSTARD SAUCE 149
SELECTION OF SALADS

PEACHES AND BUTTERSCOTCH 127
PRALINE BANANAS (x2) 127

A Lunch for 6

SUMMERY TOMATO SOUP WITH DILL 28

TAGLIATELLE WITH MUSHROOM SAUCE (x1½) 88
CARROT SALAD 134
MIXED LEAF SALAD WITH LEMONY CAPER VINAIGRETTE 147

FROZEN VANILLA MOUSSE (x2) 159
OATMEAL AND RAISIN COOKIES 177

A Romantic Dinner for 2
(halve all recipes)

EGGPLANT CAVIAR 40

VEGETABLE SOUFFLÉ 82
ROSTI 107
SPECIAL ARUGULA SALAD WITH SPINACH AND PARMESAN 129

TIRAMISÙ 162

FOR SUMMER

A Buffet for 24

GREEN HERB DIP 157
WITH CRUDITÉS

EGGPLANT CAVIAR (x2) 40

MUSHROOM
TRIANGLES (x6) 50

SUMMER LASAGNE (x2) 85

LAYERED VEGETABLE
TERRINE (x2) 81

LIGHT SPINACH AND CHEESE
PIE (x2) 113

LEMON
GREEN BEANS (x3) 44

SIMPLE
SAFFRON RICE (x2) 94

FENNEL SALAD 134

CURRIED
PASTA SALAD 144

GREEN BEAN SALAD 141

POTATO AND ROMAINE
WITH GARLIC
VINAIGRETTE 130

....

CHEESECAKE MADE WITH
STRAWBERRIES 166

CHOCOLATE MOUSSE (x2) 159

APPLE PIE 170

A Dinner Party for 8

GARDEN SOUP WITH
PESTO (x2) 26

....

MELTING EGGPLANT
(x2) 40

QUICK MEATLESS
STROGANOFF (x2) 68
WITH RICE

....

ZUCCHINI WITH
CORN (x2) 43

WATERCRESS
SALAD WITH GARLIC
CROUTONS (x2) 136

....

RASPBERRY MOUSSE 160

CRISPY GINGER SNAPS 176

An Anniversary Celebration for 12

RUSSIAN BORSCHT (x2) 22

....

CAESAR SALAD (x2) 133

....

VEGETABLE STRUDEL (x2)
110

SPINACH-FUSILLI
BAKE (x2) 92

VEGETABLE PURÉE:
CARROT (x2) 46

POTATO AND ROMAINE WITH
GARLIC VINAIGRETTE (x2)
130

....

BLUEBERRY TART (x2) 168

A Mediterranean Menu for 4

ARTICHOKE DIP 157

....

TUSCAN BEAN AND
CABBAGE SOUP 19

....

PENNE WITH TOMATOES
AND MOZZARELLA 89

PROVENÇAL PEPPER
SALAD 139

....

CHOCOLATE MOUSSE 159

MENU PLANNER

A Halloween Supper for 10

CRISPY POTATO SKINS
(x2) 105
WITH DIPS 156–7

....

PUMPKIN SOUP (x2) 20

....

BAKED CORN
PUDDING (x2) 60
MACARONI SPECIAL (x2) 93
CURRIED CHICK PEAS
WITH ONIONS (x2) 75
VEGETABLE-CHILI
RICE (x2) 97
SELECTION OF SALADS

....

APPLE PIE (x2) 170

A Brunch for 4

FRUIT JUICES 52

....

SPANISH OMELETTE 83
LIGHT SAUSAGE ROLLS 49
MEXICAN CORN BREAD 34
SERVED WITH GRILLED
TOMATOES, GRILLED
MUSHROOMS AND FRIED
BREAD

A Mexican Party for 8

GUACAMOLE 157
SALSAS 152
NACHOS 33

....

SPICY REFRIED BEAN
TACOS (x2) 35
QUESADILLAS (x8) 33
CHEESE ENCHILADAS
(x1½) 39
TACOS WITH TOMATOES
AND VEGETARIAN MINCE 34

....

ORANGE OR
LEMON SORBET 160

A Thanksgiving Dinner for 10

POTATO AND CARROT SOUP
(x1½) 17

....

MEATLESS LOAF 62
WITH YORKSHIRE
PUDDINGS 63
AND GRAVY 155
CREAMY POTATO AND
LEEK BAKE (x4) 102
ZUCCHINI WITH
CORN (x2) 43
SELECTION OF SALADS

....

PLUM COBBLER 168
CHOCOLATE DELIGHT 163

FOR AUTUMN

A Birthday Party for 6

LAYERED VEGETABLE TERRINE 81

MIXED WILD MUSHROOM SAUCE 154

SPINACH FETTUCCINE WITH CREAMY TOMATOES AND BASIL (x2) 89

LEMON GREEN BEANS (x2) 44

SPECIAL ARUGULA SALAD WITH SPINACH AND PARMESAN 129

CARROT CAKE 172 DECORATED WITH CANDLES AND FLOWERS

A Family Supper for 4

MUSHROOM TRIANGLES 50

VEGETABLE HOTCH-POTCH 61

NOODLE BAKE 60

CAESAR SALAD 133

APPLE SPONGE PUDDING 170

A Lunch for 4

CORN CHOWDER 25

CHILI NON CARNE 55

PERSIAN CHILAU RICE 96

POTATO AND ROMAINE WITH GARLIC VINAIGRETTE 130

BLUEBERRY TART 168

A Greek Menu for 6

ASPARAGUS WITH GARLIC (x1½) 44

MUSHROOM MOUSSAKA 70

GREEK RICE WITH LEEKS (x1½) 96

FENNEL SALAD 134

FROZEN MOUSSE MADE WITH GREEK YOGURT AND FRUIT (x2) 159

MENU PLANNER

A Lunch for 4

LENTIL SOUP 17

TWICE-BAKED POTATOES 101
WATERCRESS SALAD WITH GARLIC CROUTONS 136

LEMON DRIZZLE CAKE 175

An Indian Menu for 6

MUSHROOM TRIANGLES (x1½) 50
SIMPLE VEGETABLE CURRY (x2) 74
EASY CAULIFLOWER DHAL 74
POTATO AND EGGPLANT CURRY (x2) 102
CURRIED CHICK PEAS WITH ONIONS (x1½) 75
SIMPLE SAFFRON RICE (x1½) 94

MANGO SORBET 160

Two Family Suppers for 3-4

MEATLESS MEATBALLS 73
WITH SPAGHETTI AND RICH TOMATO SAUCE 151
GREEN SALAD WITH GARLIC MUSTARD DRESSING 146

BAKEWELL TART 167

CLASSIC TURNOVERS 112
RICH TOMATO SAUCE 151
TWICE-BAKED POTATOES 101
STEAMED VEGETABLES

COBBLER MADE WITH APPLES 168

A Christmas Dinner for 10

VEGETABLE SOUP (x1½) 19

COTTAGE CRUNCH CASSEROLE (x1½) 67
GRAVY 155
CHEESE AND PARSLEY SAUCE (x2) 155
SCALLOPED POTATOES (x2) 107
STEAMED VEGETABLES
ZUCCHINI WITH CORN (x3) 43
VEGETABLE PURÉE: CARROT AND PARSNIP (x1½) 46

LEMON SOUFFLÉ TART 167
CRÈME BRÛLÉE 163

FOR WINTER

A New Year's Celebration for 10

EASY LEEK PUFFS (x3) 116

SPINACH CRÊPES WITH MUSHROOMS (x2½) 79

RISOTTO (x2) 99
MADE WITH
VEGETABLES OF CHOICE

CAULIFLOWER SALAD
WITH MUSTARD
MAYONNAISE (x2) 140

BEET SALAD 140

SPONGE PUDDING WITH
APRICOTS AND ALMONDS
(x3) 171

A Dinner Party for 6

PASTA AND BEAN SALAD
WITH BASIL AND
PECORINO 142

WINTER LASAGNE 92

GREEN SALAD WITH
BALSAMIC GARLIC AND
HERB DRESSING 146

FLOATING ISLANDS 171

Sunday Lunch for 6 non-veggies

CRISPY POTATO SKINS
(x1½) 105
WITH FAVORITE DIPS

SAUSAGES BAKED IN
BATTER 63

LEMON
GREEN BEANS (x2) 44

POTATO AND CABBAGE
MASH (x2) 106

GRAVY 155

APPLE SPONGE PUDDING 170

A Dinner Party for 4

v

GREEN SOUP
WITH PARSLEY 22

CRISPY MUSHROOM
LAYERS 71

GARLIC MASHED
POTATOES 106

CARROT SALAD 134

STEAMED GREEN
VEGETABLES

FRUIT SORBET 160

VEGAN FRUIT CAKE 172

CHAPTER ONE

Soups

One of the joys of cooking without meat is making soups through the seasons, using the abundant harvest of fresh ingredients with their varied colors, flavors, and textures. The first baby vegetables appear in the spring, to enliven lighter soups; then come summer favorites like zucchini and corn. Autumn brings other squashes and globe artichokes, which make superlative soups; and winter provides root vegetables for the most warming and comforting soups of all. Spices enhance the wonderful tastes of the vegetables year round, and fresh herbs in spring and summer add qualities all their own. Whatever the season, soups can be highly nutritious as well as filling – full of vegetable protein, and rich in vitamins and minerals.

A blender or food processor is an extremely useful piece of equipment for making soups – it purées them in no time at all and with a minimum of effort. However, if you don't possess one, soups can be sieved to a smooth texture using a vegetable mill or a large wire strainer and a strong wooden spoon to push them through.

Vegetable bouillon cubes are easily obtainable, but if you prefer to make your own stock, it is an excellent way of using up vegetable scraps. A homemade stock will make soups extra tasty, too. There is a recipe on page 31.

LENTIL SOUP ᵥ

This is a really country soup, thick and warming. Adding three or four fried, sliced vegetarian sausages to this soup just before serving will turn it into a hearty main dish.

FOR 6-8

3 cups green lentils, soaked 2-3 hours	2 cans (16 ounces each) crushed tomatoes with juice
2 quarts water	2 tbsp red wine (optional)
2 tsp sea salt	2 tbsp fresh lemon juice
2 tbsp olive oil	2 tbsp brown sugar
1 large onion, chopped	2 tbsp wine vinegar
2 stalks celery, chopped	freshly ground black pepper
3 carrots, sliced	chopped fresh thyme, oregano, or basil, or chopped fresh tomatoes, for garnish
2 cloves garlic, minced	

Put the lentils in a large pan and add the water. Bring to a boil, then cover and simmer 20 minutes. Add the salt.

Meanwhile, heat the oil in another pan and cook the onion, celery, carrot, and garlic gently, covered, until soft, about 10 minutes.

Add the softened vegetables to the lentils and stir to mix. Add the tomatoes, wine if using, lemon juice, sugar, and wine vinegar. Season with pepper. Bring to a boil, then let simmer gently, uncovered, until the lentils are very tender, about 30 minutes. If the soup becomes too thick, add a little more water.

Check the seasoning and stir in chopped fresh herbs or tomatoes before serving.

POTATO AND CARROT SOUP ᵥ

A warming, comforting soup for cold weather. You can make it more substantial by sprinkling a few crisp browned vegetarian steak chunks over the top before serving – like nutritious croutons!

FOR 6

2 tbsp olive oil	skim or soy milk to thin
1 large onion, chopped	sea salt and freshly ground black pepper
2 large potatoes, peeled and diced	chopped parsley for garnish
8 large carrots, diced	
7 ½ cups vegetable stock	

Heat the oil in a large pan and cook the onion gently, covered, until soft. Add the potatoes and carrots and stir well. Pour in the stock, bring to a boil, and let cook over a low heat, partly covered, until all the vegetables are very soft and tender, 30–40 minutes.

Purée three-quarters of the soup in a blender or food processor. Mix with the remainder of the soup and reheat briefly, thinning with milk if required. Season to taste and serve hot, sprinkled with parsley.

TUSCAN BEAN AND CABBAGE SOUP ❧

This soup is nourishing and satisfying, and is delicious at any time of year, especially in cold weather. Serve with Italian bread.

FOR 6

2 tbsp olive oil	*4 tomatoes, peeled (see page 59) and chopped, or 4 canned tomatoes*
1 large onion, sliced	
2 medium carrots, thinly sliced	
2 medium turnips, thinly sliced	*2 quarts vegetable stock*
	2 tbsp chopped parsley, plus 2 tbsp chopped parsley for garnish
2-3 cloves garlic, minced	
¾ pound cabbage, shredded (about 4 cups)	
	sea salt and freshly ground black pepper
2 cans (16 ounces each) cannellini or lima beans, drained (or equivalent cooked dried, see page 185)	*grated cheese for serving (optional)*

Heat the oil in a large saucepan and cook the onion gently for 5 minutes, covered. Then add the carrots and turnips and stir until coated with oil. Stir in the garlic. Cook gently 2–3 minutes.

Stir in the remaining ingredients and bring to a boil. Cover and simmer gently until the vegetables are tender, about 25 minutes. Season to taste, and add more stock if necessary. Serve sprinkled with chopped parsley, and provide a bowl of finely grated cheese for those who want to sprinkle it on their soup.

VEGETABLE SOUP ❧

I made this soup when invited by Pierre Franey of the New York Times to be his guest on his Great Cooks TV series. It is warming winter food.

FOR 6-8

3 tbsp olive oil	*1 tsp each chopped fresh thyme and rosemary*
1 large onion, chopped	
3 leeks, thinly sliced	*5 pints vegetable stock*
1 clove garlic, minced	*8 medium tomatoes, peeled (see page 59) and chopped, or 1 can (16 ounces) crushed tomatoes with juice*
1 bunch celery, chopped	
4 large carrots, sliced	
½ small head white cabbage, shredded	*1 tbsp chopped fresh tarragon (optional)*
¾ pound new potatoes, cubed	
	sea salt and freshly ground black pepper

Heat the oil in a heavy saucepan and lightly brown the onion, leeks, garlic, and celery for 5 minutes. Add the carrots, cabbage, and potatoes and stir well. Stir in the herbs. Cover with the stock and bring to a boil. Cover and let simmer until the vegetables are tender, stirring and testing occasionally.

Add the tomatoes and tarragon (if using) and stir them in. Season to taste and heat through. Serve with warm whole-wheat rolls.

OPPOSITE: Tuscan Bean and Cabbage Soup

PARSNIP AND BUTTER BEAN SOUP

Wonderful winter food, this soup is highly nutritious, very warming, and full of flavor. Sweet parsnips make particularly delicious soups that are economical too.

FOR 4

2 tbsp olive oil	*3 ¾ cups vegetable stock*
1 large onion, chopped	*1 bay leaf*
3 large cloves garlic, sliced	*1 tbsp fresh lemon juice*
2 large parsnips, washed and chopped	*⅓ cup crème fraîche or light cream*
3 medium potatoes, washed and chopped	*2 ½ cups skim or soy milk*
1 can (16 ounces) butter or lima beans (or equivalent cooked dried, see page 185)	*sea salt and freshly ground black pepper*

Heat the oil in a heavy saucepan and stir in the onion and garlic. Cover and cook gently until softened, 8–10 minutes. Add the chopped parsnips and potatoes and stir well, then add the butter or lima beans with the juices from the can. Pour in the vegetable stock and add the bay leaf and lemon juice. Bring to a boil, then cover and let simmer very gently until the vegetables are completely softened, 20–25 minutes.

Discard the bay leaf, then purée the soup in a blender or food processor, with the crème fraîche or cream. Thin with the milk. Season to taste, and reheat gently for serving.

PUMPKIN SOUP ♥

The vibrant color of this soup – orange with small flecks of green – will cheer and warm on a chilly day. You can toast the pumpkin seeds and use them to garnish the soup (the shells of the seeds are edible although tough).

FOR 6

1 ¾-pound piece of pumpkin, peeled, seeds and fibers removed and flesh cut into cubes (about 4 cups)	*2 tbsp olive oil*
	2 onions, chopped
	¾ cup chopped parsley
1 ½ quarts water	*sea salt and freshly ground black pepper*

In a large saucepan, simmer the pumpkin cubes in the water until they are very tender.

Meanwhile, heat the oil in a frying pan and sauté the onions until golden.

Purée the pumpkin and liquid in a blender or food processor, or press through a strainer, and return to the pan. Add the sautéed onions and the parsley. Season to taste and heat through.

OPPOSITE: Parsnip and Butter Bean Soup

RUSSIAN BORSCHT ❧

This famous soup from Russia is hearty and satisfying, a warming soup for winter weather. You can make a meal of it, served with warm whole-wheat or rye bread.

FOR 6

6 large beets, peeled	5 pints vegetable stock
1 potato, peeled	2 tbsp fresh lemon juice
1 large onion, chopped	salt and freshly ground black pepper
2 tbsp olive oil	
2 ½ cups green cabbage cut in fine matchsticks	⅔ cup sour cream (optional)
	chopped fresh dill or parsley for garnish
¼ pound tomatoes, peeled (see page 59) and chopped (about ½ cup)	

Slice the beets and potato very finely, then cut the slices into matchsticks. Brown the onion lightly in the oil for 3–4 minutes, then add the rest of the vegetables and stir together for several minutes. Pour in enough stock to cover and bring to a boil. Simmer until tender, 20–30 minutes.

Add the rest of the stock and the lemon juice. Purée half of the soup in a blender or food processor, then return it to the remaining soup in the pan and reheat gently. Season to taste. Put a dollop of sour cream on each bowl of soup (vegans can omit this) and garnish with chopped dill or parsley.

GREEN SOUP WITH PARSLEY ❧

The celery flavor in this soup is highlighted by the subtle taste of split peas. It is a deliciously wholesome soup, perfect for cold weather.

FOR 4

¾ cup dried split peas	1 bay leaf
2 tbsp olive oil	3 ¾ cups vegetable stock
1 medium onion, chopped	sea salt and freshly ground black pepper
4 stalks celery, sliced	
2 carrots, sliced	chopped parsley for garnish
¼ cup chopped parsley	

Cover the split peas with hot water and let soak 1 hour. Drain and set to one side.

Heat the oil in a large saucepan and sauté the onion for 3–4 minutes. Add the celery and carrots and cook over medium heat until lightly browned. Add the drained split peas, the parsley, and bay leaf. Pour in the stock and stir well. Cover the pan and bring to a boil, then let simmer until the split peas are very tender, 1–1½ hours. Add more water or vegetable stock if required as the soup cooks.

Season to taste and serve immediately, sprinkled with chopped parsley.

OPPOSITE: Russian Borscht

CORN CHOWDER

A great American classic, this creamy, golden soup is easy to make and a treat at any time of the year. Its texture is as satisfying as its flavors.

FOR 4

1 very large potato or 2 small potatoes, peeled and cut in ½-inch cubes	2 cups milk
2 cups water	½ cup light cream
1 onion, chopped	sea salt and freshly ground black pepper
2 tbsp olive oil	paprika to taste
3 cups fresh corn kernels stripped from about 6 ears of corn (see page 34), or 2 cans (16 ounces each) whole kernel corn	pinch of dried thyme
	1 bay leaf
	freshly chopped parsley and chives to taste

Parboil the potato in the water about 10 minutes. Meanwhile, cook the onion in the oil over low heat, covered, until translucent, 5–8 minutes. Add the onion and the remaining ingredients to the potatoes and bring back to a boil. Let simmer until the corn is tender and the soup is slightly thickened, 20–30 minutes, stirring occasionally. Discard the bay leaf before serving.

ASPARAGUS SOUP

T he delicate flavor of asparagus comes through well in this attractive pale green soup. If fresh asparagus is not in season, you can substitute canned – the result will be just as delicious.

FOR 4

2 tbsp vegetable oil	½ pound fresh asparagus, tough ends removed, chopped, or equivalent canned asparagus, drained and chopped
1 onion, chopped	
1 medium potato, peeled and diced	
4 stalks celery, chopped	sea salt and freshly ground black pepper
2 ½ cups vegetable stock	milk to thin the soup if necessary

In a large saucepan, heat the oil and cook the onion until soft and translucent. Add the potato and celery and cook for a further 2 minutes, stirring. Pour in half the stock and bring to a boil, then cover and simmer until the potatoes are tender, 10–15 minutes.

Add the asparagus and the remaining stock. Cover again and cook until all the vegetables are tender, about 10 minutes longer.

Ladle half of the vegetables into a blender or food processor and purée. Return to the pan and stir to mix with the remainder of the soup and vegetables. Season to taste and heat through. If the soup is too thick, thin with a little milk.

OPPOSITE: Corn Chowder

GARDEN SOUP WITH PESTO ⱽ

*U*tilizing the early summer vegetables from the garden makes this a light, refreshing soup. It is so pretty to look at, too, with its contrasting colours. Vegans can omit the garnish of cheese.

FOR 4–6

3 tbsp olive oil	*1 small head crisp lettuce, shredded*
1 clove garlic, minced	
1 medium leek, thinly sliced	*1 tbsp chopped fresh tarragon*
2 large carrots, diced	*²/₃ cup simple pesto sauce (see page 149)*
1 small turnip, diced	
2 small potatoes, peeled and diced	*sea salt and freshly ground black pepper*
5 cups vegetable stock	*grated cheese for serving (optional)*
1 cup frozen green peas, thawed	

Heat the olive oil in a large saucepan and sauté the garlic, leek, carrots, turnip, and potatoes until they are beginning to soften, 5–6 minutes. Pour in the stock and bring to a boil, then let simmer until the vegetables are tender, 15–20 minutes.

Add the peas and lettuce and simmer 5 minutes more. Stir in the tarragon and pesto and season to taste. Serve with a bowl of freshly grated cheese.

ZUCCHINI AND WATERCRESS SOUP ⱽ

*T*his lovely green soup has a distinctive, subtle flavor and is a treat served with hot garlic bread, or with croutons for a contrasting crunch. If you want a creamy, non-vegan version, add some crème fraîche or thick plain yogurt.

FOR 4–6

3 tbsp olive oil	*2 bunches watercress, stems trimmed*
2 large mild onions, finely sliced	
	sea salt and freshly ground black pepper
5 cups vegetable stock	
2 pounds zucchini, trimmed and roughly chopped	*fresh lemon juice*

Heat the oil in a heavy saucepan and stir in the sliced onions. Cover and cook them over low heat until tender and sweet, 10–15 minutes. Add the stock and bring to a boil, then add the zucchini. Simmer, uncovered, until they are very tender, about 15 minutes. Remove from the heat.

Add the watercress to the pan, stir well, and cover. Let stand 5 minutes.

Strain through a large strainer set in a bowl. Set the liquid aside and purée the solids in a blender or food processor, or press them through the strainer, until perfectly smooth. Return them to the pan and stir in the liquid. Reheat gently. Season to taste and add a little lemon juice to sharpen the flavor. Serve at once.

OPPOSITE: Garden Soup with Pesto

GAZPACHO ANDALUZ ⌄

A wonderful chilled soup, with refreshing tastes, full of natural vitamins. Serve in small bowls with the garnishes to pass around.

FOR 6

2 slices whole-wheat bread, crusts removed	*2 canned pimientos, drained and chopped, or 1 large fresh red bell pepper, chopped*
2 tbsp olive oil	
3 tbsp fresh lemon juice	*6 green onions, roughly chopped*
3 cloves garlic, minced	*½ hothouse cucumber, roughly chopped*
1½ pounds large tomatoes, peeled (see page 59) and chopped, or 1 can (28 ounces) tomatoes, drained and chopped	*2 cups tomato juice*
	sea salt and freshly ground black pepper
	2–3 tbsp mayonnaise (optional)

For the garnish a selection from:

pitted black olives	*finely diced raw onion*
finely diced cucumber	*finely chopped tomatoes*
chopped green bell pepper (or red or yellow)	*minced parsley*
small cubes of toasted or fried bread	

Soak the bread in the olive oil and lemon juice, with the garlic, while you prepare the vegetables.

Put everything, apart from the seasoning and mayonnaise, into the blender and run until smooth. Season to taste and stir in the mayonnaise, if using. Chill thoroughly before serving, with the garnishes.

SUMMERY TOMATO SOUP WITH DILL ⌄

A fresh, summery soup, ideal served chilled for lunch on a warm day. Use home-grown tomatoes in full season for the best flavor.

FOR 4–6

¼ cup olive oil	*1 tsp ground allspice (optional)*
2 large onions, finely sliced	
2 large cloves garlic, minced	*pinch of sugar (optional)*
large bunch of fresh dill, chopped	*sea salt and freshly ground black pepper*
7½ cups vegetable stock	*finely grated rind of ½ orange*
1 can (28 ounces) tomatoes, or 1½ pounds fresh tomatoes, peeled (see page 59) and chopped	*½ cup sour cream (optional)*
	sprigs of fresh dill for garnish

Heat the oil in a saucepan and stir in the onions. Cover and cook gently, stirring occasionally, until completely soft and sweet, about 10 minutes.

Add the garlic and cook, covered, for 5 minutes longer. Stir in half of the dill and cook, uncovered, for 3–4 minutes more.

Pour in the vegetable stock and add the canned tomatoes with their juice or the chopped fresh tomatoes and the optional allspice and sugar. Season with salt and pepper. Bring to a boil and let simmer gently 35–40 minutes.

Add the orange rind. Remove from the heat and let cool slightly. Purée the soup, in batches, in a blender or food processor until it is quite smooth. Add the remaining dill. Return it to the pan, unless serving cold, and heat through very gently for 5 minutes. Correct the seasoning and serve, with a dollop of sour cream on each serving, if desired, and garnished with a sprig of dill.

OPPOSITE: Gazpacho Andaluz

THICK ARTICHOKE SOUP

This simple soup has the most amazing flavor, and is a meal in itself with warm whole-wheat rolls. Serve it with croutons, too, if you want a contrasting crunch.

FOR 4

2 pounds Jerusalem artichokes, peeled	*1 tbsp olive oil*
5 cups vegetable stock	*⅓ cup crème fraîche or light cream*
½ onion, chopped	*sea salt and freshly ground black pepper*

Put the artichokes in a saucepan, cover with cold water, and bring to a boil. Cover and simmer until completely soft. Cool in the liquid, then drain.

Turn the artichokes into a blender or food processor, add half of the vegetable stock, and purée until smooth, then gradually add the rest of the stock. Alternatively, press the artichokes through a strainer and stir in the stock.

Cook the onion in the oil until translucent. Meanwhile, reheat the soup, then stir in the onion and crème fraîche or cream and season to taste.

CROUTONS

Add lovely munchy croutons to soups for extra texture or for a more filling meal. Using the optional garlic makes the croutons even tastier.

FOR 4

4 medium slices bread, crusts removed	*1 large clove garlic, minced (optional)*
vegetable oil for frying	

Cut the crustless slices of bread into tiny cubes. Heat the oil gently in a frying pan and fry the bread cubes over medium heat, shaking to turn them until they begin to turn golden and crisp. Add the garlic, if using, towards the end of cooking, keeping the heat down to prevent the garlic from burning. Stir the garlic croutons thoroughly.

When evenly browned – and be careful not to overcook them – remove the croutons from the pan with a slotted spoon and drain on paper towels.

Keep in a warm oven until ready to serve.

VEGETABLE STOCK ᵛ

This is the basis of many soups. It can be made whenever you have vegetable scraps or peelings at hand and stored in the refrigerator. It is worth getting into the habit of making vegetable stock regularly, so that you always have some when you need it.

MAKES as much as you like!

vegetable scraps, such as onion, carrot, leek, cabbage, tomato, broccoli, cauliflower, Jerusalem artichoke, potato peelings	*sea salt*
	black peppercorns
	bay leaves
	fresh herbs in season or dried herbs
cold water to cover	

Put the vegetable scraps or trimmings into a large saucepan and cover with cold water. Add a little sea salt, a sprinkling of black peppercorns and a couple of bay leaves for flavor. Add a small bunch of fresh herbs – such as sage, parsley, thyme, chives and/or tarragon – according to season, or a tablespoon or so of dried mixed herbs.

Bring to a boil and simmer, covered, for 45 minutes. Then let stand until cold.

Strain, and store in the refrigerator for up to 5 days.

DUMPLINGS ᵛ

Dumplings are a mainstay of the family cook, and they always WERE meatless, although of course you need to use vegetable suet to make them vegetarian. Simply cook them in simmering vegetable stock (above) and serve them with any of your favorite meatless meals. You can also make them using whole-wheat flour, or half white and half whole-wheat.

MAKES 8

¾ cup all-purpose flour	*sea salt and freshly ground black pepper*
¼ cup shredded vegetable suet	

Mix the flour with the suet and some salt and pepper, then add enough cold water to mix to an elastic dough. Shape into 8 dumplings and cook in simmering stock for 20–25 minutes.

VARIATIONS

To the basic mixture add one of the following:
- 1 tbsp each grated Parmesan cheese and chopped parsley
- 1 tbsp dried mixed herbs of your choice
- 1 tbsp each grated cheese and chopped fresh chives
- 1 tbsp chopped fresh basil
- 1 tbsp grated cheese

CHAPTER TWO

Light Meals and Side Dishes

Within this section you'll find an exciting range of snacks, appetizers, and side dishes that you can make quickly and easily – from tempting nibbles to go with a drink before a meal, such as crisp and succulent cheese palmiers, to classic dishes like vegetable tempura, which always looks so amazing on the plate and is loved by everybody.

The selection of Mexican recipes here demonstrates the versatility of the tortilla, the Mexican crêpe, which is used in tacos, enchiladas, burritos, and nachos. All of these make wonderful and satisfying quick meals. They are highly nutritious because they often contain refried beans or vegetarian mince, as well as good supplies of carbohydrates. Lightly spiced with chile peppers, these irresistible dishes deserve to become part of every family cook's repertoire.

MEXICAN SNACK FOODS

THE VERSATILE TORTILLA

Tortillas are the Mexican version of crêpes, made of wheat flour or cornmeal (masa harina). They are the basis of tacos, burritos, enchiladas, nachos, and quesadillas. You can buy tortillas ready-made.

Tacos are cornmeal tortillas folded in half and fried crisp. You can buy tacos, or you can make your own tortilla shells by frying tortillas, using a ladle to make a hollow in the center (see page 35). Use your imagination and any fillings inspired by favorite recipes in this book to make wonderful snacks. For authentic Mexican flavor add canned mild chiles to your mixture – they will not blow your head off as fresh chiles are apt to do!

BURRITOS AND CHIMICHANGAS

A burrito is a warm flour tortilla filled with cooked vegetables (often including beans or refried beans), folded into a parcel with shredded cheese, and topped with salad. Zucchini, broccoli, snow peas, carrots, and spinach all make excellent fillings and go well with the shredded cheese.

Put the filling of cooked vegetables, beans, shredded cheese, and shredded salad into the center of the warm tortilla, fold the bottom quarter over, then the sides, and then the top, to make an "envelope." Serve immediately.

For a chimichanga, simply fry the filled burrito in shallow oil until golden brown. Serve with a Mexican salsa (for homemade versions, see page 152), guacamole (page 157), or sour cream.

QUESADILLAS

A quesadilla is a turnover, made with a flour tortilla and fried lightly in oil. Here, refried beans and cheese provide the filling.

FOR 1 (MAKES 2)

2 small flour tortillas	*2 heaped tbsp bottled taco*
¼ cup canned refried beans,	*sauce or homemade salsa (see*
thinned out with a little water	*page 152)*
2 ounces mild cheddar or	*sliced fresh hot chile pepper*
Monterey Jack cheese, thinly	*(optional)*
sliced	*vegetable oil for frying*

Spread the tortillas with the refried bean mixture and place the sliced cheese on top. Dot the taco sauce or salsa on the cheese and add a slice or two of fresh chile pepper if you like hot spicing.

Fold the tortillas into crescent shapes and fry in a very little oil in a hot pan until browned on both sides and heated through. Serve immediately.

NACHOS

These are fantastic! If your family is hungry and looking for a very fast snack, make these nibbles instead of opening a bag of potato chips.

FOR 6–8

5 ounces tortilla chips	*½ cup bottled taco sauce*
2 cups shredded mild cheddar	*(optional)*
or Monterey Jack cheese	

Spread the tortilla chips one layer deep on baking sheets. Sprinkle with the cheese and dot the sauce over the top. Bake in a preheated 400°F oven for 5 minutes. Serve immediately and eat at once!

MEXICAN CORN BREAD

*T*his is nothing less than beautiful – spicy and deliciously cheesy! Serve it warm from the oven, or reheat slices in the microwave for 30 seconds (this will retain its tender crumb and moistness).

FOR 4–6

1 free-range egg	½ cup crème fraîche or sour cream
2 tbsp olive oil	
1-2 tbsp minced fresh hot chile pepper	1 cup yellow cornmeal
	1 tsp sea salt
1 cup canned whole kernel corn, drained, or 2-3 fresh ears of corn, kernels stripped off (see right)	1 tsp baking powder
	2 cups grated cheddar cheese

Beat the egg with the oil until blended. Add the chile pepper. Stir in the corn, crème fraîche, cornmeal, salt, baking powder, and all but ½ cup of the cheese. Pour into an 8- or 9-inch square pan. Sprinkle the remaining cheese over the top.

Bake in a preheated 350°F oven for 40 minutes. Let cool slightly in the pan, then unmold and serve warm.

Stripping Corn Kernels off the Cob

Remove the outer leaves or husks and all silk from the corn. Holding the corn cob upright with the flat end firmly on a board, run a sharp knife down the length, between the kernels and the cob, to strip the kernels away.

TACOS WITH TOMATOES AND VEGETARIAN MINCE ᵛ

*T*his is a really tasty snack meal with an appetizing mixture of textures, flavors, and colors. Vegans can make these omitting the cheese topping.

MAKES 8

3 ¼ cups vegetarian mince	sea salt and freshly ground black pepper
2 tbsp olive oil	
⅓ cup chopped almonds	1-2 tsp cayenne pepper or to taste
2 small onions, thinly sliced	
2 cloves garlic, thinly sliced	8 taco shells, warmed
3 tomatoes, peeled (see page 59) and chopped (fresh or canned)	¾ cup shredded cheddar cheese (optional)
	shredded lettuce
a little tomato juice to bind	

Brown the vegetarian mince in 1 tbsp oil for 3–4 minutes, then add the almonds and cook until they are browned too. In a separate pan, soften the onions and garlic in the rest of the oil. Stir in the tomatoes with a little tomato juice and cook until well amalgamated. Season to taste with salt, pepper, and cayenne. Add the vegetarian mince and almond mixture and stir well.

Fill the warm taco shells. Top with shredded cheese and shredded lettuce. Serve with the no-cook salsa or the chili sauce on page 152.

SPICY REFRIED BEAN TACOS ⱱ

*R*ich and filling, a snack for the hungry! Crisp taco shells are filled with a spicy tomato and bean mixture, shredded lettuce, and grated cheese, and topped with sliced avocado and sour cream. (Vegans can omit the cheese and sour cream.)

MAKES 4

1 cup canned refried beans	1-2 tsp hot chili sauce or to taste
2-3 tbsp bottled taco sauce or homemade salsa (see page 152)	sea salt
	4 taco shells, warmed
4 medium tomatoes, peeled (see page 59) and chopped	shredded mild cheese (optional)
4 green onions, thinly sliced	shredded lettuce

For garnish:

sliced avocado	sour cream (optional)

Heat the refried beans with the taco sauce. Add the chopped tomatoes and mash thoroughly. Add the green onions and cook gently for 4–5 minutes, stirring frequently. Season to taste with chili sauce and a little salt if desired.

Half-fill the warm taco shells with the mixture and top with shredded cheese and shredded lettuce (you can put the lettuce at the bottom of the shell if you prefer). Garnish with a slice or two of avocado and a dollop of sour cream.

BEAN TACOS WITH RED BELL PEPPERS ⱱ

*M*emorable tastes that linger on the palate and make a snack meal with a difference. As with the other tacos, vegans can eat these if they omit the cheese and sour cream.

MAKES 8

1 tbsp olive oil	⅓ cup chili sauce
1 onion, sliced	1 head iceberg lettuce, shredded
1 red bell pepper, seeded and chopped	8 taco shells, warmed
1 can (16 ounces) pinto or red kidney beans, drained (or equivalent cooked dried beans, see page 185)	¾ cup shredded cheddar or Monterey Jack cheese
	sour cream

Heat the oil and soften the onion and bell pepper for 5 minutes. Add the beans and cook uncovered for 10 minutes. Mash, and then mix in the chili sauce.

Put shredded lettuce into the warm taco shells, spoon the warm bean mixture over the top, and top with cheese and sour cream.

Tortilla shells

Deep fry a cornmeal tortilla in very hot oil, pushing the center down with a ladle. Cook until golden – half a minute or so. Remove the ladle and let the tortilla finish cooking until golden. Drain on paper towels and dry. Stuff with any of the fillings above, top with shredded cheese, and finish with shredded salad.

NEXT SPREAD: A Mexican feast with, left to right, Sour Cream Enchiladas with Tomato and Chili Salsa (see page 152) on the side, Corn Bread, Tortillas piled with mixed vegetables, and Guacamole (see page 157)

ENCHILADAS

*E*nchiladas are the Mexican equivalent of a stuffed crêpe – flour tortillas are rolled up around a tasty filling and then baked, often topped with a spicy sauce.

TRADITIONAL ENCHILADAS

A tasty dish that is highly nutritious. The creamy vegetarian-mince filling is rolled up inside tortillas, which are baked until crisp. Serve a salad of crisp green leaves and orange segments alongside, for a refreshing contrast.

MAKES 4

2 cups vegetarian mince	½ cup crème fraîche or sour cream
2 tbsp vegetable oil	
½ small onion, chopped	1-2 tsp chili powder or to taste
1 cup shredded cheddar or Monterey Jack cheese	4 flour tortillas

Sauté the vegetarian mince in the oil. Mix with the onion, cheese, crème fraîche, and chili powder and use to fill the tortillas. Roll them up and bake, seam-side down, in a preheated 375°F oven until hot through and crisp on top, 15–20 minutes.

Chiles

Chiles come from a large botanical family with many varieties. You see them in all sizes and colors – red, green, cream and even purple. The plump green jalapeño chile is popular and used in many Mexican dishes. Chiles vary in strength quite considerably so it is prudent to err on the side of caution when adding them to your recipe: start with a little and then add to taste.

Dried chiles are a useful standby in the kitchen pantry, and can be very hot. Canned chiles, however, tend to be milder and are a truly delicious way of spicing. Beware of chiles in vinegar – they blow your head off.

SOUR CREAM ENCHILADAS

These are rich and succulent, and are just the thing for a casual summer meal with friends, served with a tossed salad. To make the meal more substantial, add Mexican rice 'n' beans or the vegetable-chili rice on page 97.

MAKES 6

6 flour tortillas	*1 cup shredded mild cheddar cheese*
¼ cup salsa (see page 152) or light tomato sauce (see page 151)	*1¼ cups sour cream*
⅔ cup chopped onion	*olives for garnish*

Brush the surface of each tortilla with some salsa or tomato sauce. Mix the chopped onion with the shredded cheese and half of the sour cream. Put this filling into the center of the tortillas and roll them up. Place seam-side down in a baking dish. Cover with the rest of the sour cream, and bake in a preheated 375°F oven until golden, about 20 minutes.

Garnish with olives and serve with more salsa or tomato sauce.

CHEESE ENCHILADAS

This is a wonderfully simple snack meal, or it can be a light supper served with rice and a salad such as the watercress salad with garlic croutons on page 30 or carrot salad (see page 134).

MAKES 6

3 tbsp corn relish	*4 canned tomatoes, drained and chopped*
1 cup shredded cheddar cheese	*3 green onions, chopped*
1 cup shredded iceberg lettuce	*6 flour tortillas*
	6 tbsp sour cream (optional)

Mix together the corn relish, cheese, lettuce, tomatoes and green onions and roll up inside the tortillas. Bake, seam-side down, in a preheated 375°F oven until the tops of the tortillas are crisp and lightly browned, about 20 minutes. Top with sour cream, if using.

MELTING EGGPLANT WITH BELL PEPPERS

*T*his makes an excellent light lunch or supper dish, or you can serve it as a first course for a more formal meal. A glass of red wine and crusty whole-wheat bread will complete the menu.

FOR 4

2 medium eggplants, cut in thick slices	*½ pound soft goat cheese or any soft cheese, sliced*
3 tbsp olive oil	*freshly ground black pepper*
2 canned pimientos, drained and quartered, or 1 large fresh red bell pepper, peeled (see page 59) and quartered	*pitted olives for garnish*

Sprinkle the slices of eggplant with a touch of salt. Brush them with olive oil and place on a large baking sheet. Bake in a preheated 425°F oven until soft and golden brown, 10–12 minutes.

Layer the eggplant slices, pimientos, and goat cheese in four or eight stacks on a baking sheet, seasoning with freshly ground black pepper as you go along. Top each stack with a piece of cheese. Return to the oven and bake 5 minutes to heat through. Garnish with a pitted olive or two, and serve immediately.

EGGPLANT CAVIAR ♥

*T*his Middle-Eastern dip is also known as "poor man's caviar," although it is just as luxurious as the real thing. Serve with toasted triangles of pita bread or carrot sticks.

FOR 4

2 large eggplants	*1 large clove garlic, minced*
juice of 2-3 lemons	*sea salt*
2 ½ tbsp tahini (sesame paste)	*¼ cup chopped parsley*
3 tbsp sesame seeds	*1 tbsp olive oil*

Pierce the eggplants several times with a sharp knife. Bake in a preheated 375°F oven until soft, 30–40 minutes. Set aside to cool for about 30 minutes.

Peel the eggplants and discard the skin. Put the flesh in a bowl and immediately add the lemon juice. Mash well or blend in a food processor. Add the tahini, sesame seeds, and garlic and mix in thoroughly. Season with salt.

Spoon into a serving dish, cover, and chill. Before serving, sprinkle with the parsley and drizzle the olive oil over the top.

OPPOSITE: Melting Eggplants with Bell Peppers

LIGHT VEGETABLE TEMPURA

Tempura from Japan makes one of the best snack meals in the world. Lovely with a sweet and sour sauce (see page 153), the chili sauce on page 152, or the tamari sauce here, and served with boiled rice.

FOR 4

½ pound zucchini, thickly sliced	For the batter:
	¾ cup all-purpose flour
½ pound small button mushrooms	*1 free-range egg*
	scant cup water
½ pound broccoli florets (about 2 heaped cups)	*⅛ tsp sea salt*
	Optional sauce:
¼ pound cauliflower florets (about 1 heaped cup)	*4 tbsp tamari sauce*
vegetable oil for deep-frying	*grated fresh ginger and green onion to taste*

Prepare the vegetables. Put the batter ingredients into the blender or food processor and purée until smooth. It is now ready to use.

Make the sauce you intend to use. Set aside.

Pour the oil about 3 inches deep into a large saucepan. Heat to 325°F.

Dip the pieces of vegetable in the batter one at a time and place carefully in the hot oil. Do not fry too many pieces at once. Fry the vegetables, turning them over occasionally, until they are lightly golden all over – each batch takes a couple of minutes. Lift out and put on paper towels to drain. Keep the tempura hot in a warm oven while you fry the next batch. When all are fried, serve without delay.

ZUCCHINI WITH CORN ▼

This simple recipe is easily prepared, and its colors are delightful – yellow, and green glow on the plate. Serve with the saffron rice on page 94 or with plain noodles and a tossed salad.

FOR 3-4

2 tbsp olive oil	*small handful of fresh tarragon, chopped, or 1 tbsp dried tarragon*
1 pound zucchini, cubed (about 3 ½ cups)	
2 cups canned whole kernel corn, drained	*sea salt and freshly ground black pepper*
1 small onion, chopped	
1 large clove garlic, minced	

Heat the oil in a large frying pan and add all the ingredients. Cook gently, stirring, until they begin to soften, about 5 minutes. Then cover with a lid and cook over very low heat for 5 minutes more.

Check the seasoning and serve hot.

OPPOSITE: Light Vegetable Tempura with Chili Sauce

ASPARAGUS WITH GARLIC

When asparagus is in season, make the most of it and try this unusual way of serving it, with garlic-flavored oil, lemon juice, and freshly grated Parmesan.

FOR 4

2-3 cloves garlic, minced	½ cup grated Parmesan cheese
4 tbsp olive oil	2 tsp fresh lemon juice
2 pounds asparagus	

Mix minced garlic to taste with the oil and set aside. Stand the asparagus spears upright in a tall pan of boiling water (the tips should not be submerged), cover, and cook until tender, 8–10 minutes. Lift the asparagus carefully into a colander to drain.

Arrange the asparagus on warm plates and spoon the garlic oil over the tips. Sprinkle with grated Parmesan cheese and lemon juice and serve immediately, with warm crusty bread to mop up the juices.

LEMON GREEN BEANS ❧

With broiled tomatoes and pita bread, this fresh-tasting vegetable dish will make a lovely light meal. Or, you can serve it to accompany a main dish such as the baked corn pudding on page 60.

FOR 3–4

½ pound thin green beans	sea salt and freshly ground
4 tbsp margarine	black pepper
3 tbsp fresh lemon juice	3 tbsp chopped parsley

Steam the beans until crisp-tender, 3–4 minutes. Melt the margarine in a pan and stir in the beans. Cover and cook over medium-low heat until tender, about 5 minutes.

Add the lemon juice and season to taste. Cook for a further 3 minutes, then sprinkle on the parsley. Mix well, and put into a serving dish.

Steaming

Cooking vegetables in a steamer conserves their valuable vitamins and minerals, and retains their full flavor. Vegetables can be steamed either whole, sliced or chopped. Time allowed depends on the size and type of vegetable and whether you wish to cook them to softness or 'al dente' slightly crisp. Steamers can be bought at all good kitchen stores.

Cooking vegetables in a microwave oven is also in effect steaming them: covered with plastic wrap, with a little water added, this method also brings out the full flavor of the vegetables while retaining their goodness.

OPPOSITE: Asparagus with Garlic (top) and Lemon Green Beans

VEGETABLE PURÉES

*Y*ou can adapt this recipe, with broccoli, to make many other vegetable purées, such as carrot, Brussels sprout, cauliflower, zucchini, pumpkin, potato with celery root, parsnip, cabbage, and rutabaga. Two other variations are suggested below.

FOR 6

2 pounds broccoli, trimmed and chopped	*½ cup grated cheese*
⅔ cup crème fraîche or light cream	*½ tsp each grated nutmeg and freshly ground black pepper*
	sea salt
¼ cup sour cream	*2 tbsp margarine (optional)*

Steam the broccoli until tender, 8–10 minutes. Put it into a food processor with the crème fraîche or cream and purée thoroughly, or press through a strainer. Stir in the sour cream and grated cheese. Add the nutmeg, pepper, and salt to taste.

FOR LEEK AND POTATO PURÉE: Cook 1½ pounds potatoes, peeled, and 6 large leeks, sliced, in separate pans of boiling salted water until tender. Drain well, reserving the cooking liquid from the leeks. Soften 2 cloves garlic, sliced finely, in 3 tbsp olive oil; add the leeks and cook gently for 10 minutes. Meanwhile, purée the potatoes in a blender or food processor with ⅔ cup crème fraîche or light cream (vegans can use tofu instead). Add the leek and garlic mixture and run the machine again until the purée is completely smooth, adding some of the reserved leek cooking liquid to thin to the desired consistency. Season to taste, and reheat gently before serving.

FOR CREAMED SPINACH: Steam 2 pounds fresh spinach, trimmed, until tender, then drain well, pressing out all excess liquid. Chop the spinach or work in a food processor until quite fine. Heat 1 tbsp butter or olive oil in a pan, add the spinach, and heat through, stirring. Stir in ⅔ cup crème fraîche or light cream. Season to taste.

CHEESE AND NUT PÂTÉ

*C*runchy and garlicky, this pâté makes a great start to a meal, or a light luncheon dish in its own right with a tossed salad, such as the special arugula salad on page 129.

FOR 4

1 slice whole-wheat bread, crusts removed	*¾ cup shredded cheddar cheese*
6 tbsp skim milk or soy milk	*1 large clove garlic, minced*
1 cup walnut or pecan pieces	*2 tbsp olive oil*
	freshly ground black pepper
	sprigs of parsley for garnish

Soak the bread in the milk. Blend the nuts roughly in a food processor – not too smooth because you want the pâté to have texture. With a fork, work the nuts, cheese, garlic, and oil into the soaked bread. Season with lots of pepper. Press into a mold or terrine, and chill.

To serve, unmold and garnish with sprigs of parsley. Eat with thin slices of toast or baby tomatoes, celery and carrot sticks, and a selection of other crudités in season.

BELOW: Cheese and Nut Pâté

CHEESE PALMIERS

These light cheese-filled pastries just melt in the mouth. Perfect as an appetizer to nibble before a meal, you'll find that they disappear like the melting snow.

MAKES 20

½ pound frozen or homemade puff pastry (see page 178)

½ pound cheddar cheese, shredded (about 2 cups)

paprika

Roll out the pastry thinly into a rectangle. Cover thickly with the cheese and press it down well. Sprinkle generously with paprika.

Fold one long edge of the pastry into the center. Moisten the upper side of the edge with water. Fold the other long edge into the center and press down to seal the edges together. Cut into ¼-inch slices. Lay them, cut-side down, on a well-greased baking sheet.

Bake in a preheated 425°F oven until golden brown, about 20 minutes. Let cool on a wire rack for 5 minutes, and they are ready to serve.

FILO CHEESE STRAWS

These "cigars" are a variation on the theme of cheese straws, and they really are irresistible, so you probably need to make more than you expect! Use a cheese with a good, strong flavor.

MAKES 12–14

¼ pound filo pastry

olive oil

1½ cups shredded cheese

freshly ground black pepper

Cut the filo sheets in half crosswise. Brush each one with olive oil, then fold in half and brush with oil again. Place a narrow band of shredded cheese along one long edge and grind black pepper over the top. Roll up tightly. Cut the roll in half and brush the top with olive oil. Repeat with the remaining filo sheets. Place on a greased baking sheet and bake in a preheated 425°F oven for 15 minutes. Eat hot, or while still warm.

LIGHT SAUSAGE ROLLS ∨

*T*hese are so satisfying that any would-be meat eaters will love them! The first version wraps the vegetarian sausages in puff pastry, while the second uses crisp filo pastry. Vegans can omit the egg-yolk coating or cheese.

MAKES 8

8 large vegetarian sausage links	*1 free-range egg yolk, beaten*
½ pound frozen or homemade puff pastry (see page 78)	

Broil or fry the vegetarian sausages as instructed on the package. Let cool.

Roll out the pastry fairly thinly and cut into eight rectangles that are the length of the sausages. Roll up a sausage in each rectangle so that the pastry just overlaps, and put seam-side down on a greased baking sheet. Score the top with a sharp knife, making long diagonal lines. Brush with beaten egg yolk and bake in a preheated 400°F oven until the pastry is puffed and golden, about 25 minutes.

MAKES 8

8 small vegetarian sausage links	*olive oil*
8 sheets filo pastry	*8 slivers hard well-flavored cheese*

Broil or fry the vegetarian sausages as instructed on the package. Let cool.

Cut each sheet of filo pastry in half. Brush the pieces of filo with olive oil and fold each one in half. Brush with oil again. Roll up a sausage and a sliver of cheese in a folded piece of filo, then roll up each roll in the remaining folded pieces of filo. Brush the tops of the rolls with more olive oil and place on a greased baking sheet. Bake in a preheated 400°F oven until golden, about 20 minutes.

PARTY EGGS

*Y*ou can vary the flavors in this recipe by using different relishes – corn or tomato, for example – and curry powder instead of paprika. Feel free to improvise!

FOR 6

6 free-range eggs	*sea salt and freshly ground black pepper*
⅓-½ cup bottled or homemade mayonnaise (see page 150)	*paprika*
1 tsp mild mustard or more to taste	
2½ tbsp sweet pickle relish (optional)	*For garnish:*
	sliced pitted olives or capers
	sprigs of parsley

Hard-boil the eggs for 10 minutes. Drain the eggs and plunge into cold water. Let cool.

When the eggs are cold, peel them carefully. Cut in half lengthwise and scoop out the yolks into a bowl. Mash the yolks with the mayonnaise, mustard, and relish if using. Season to taste with salt, pepper, and paprika.

Pile the mixture back into the egg whites. Arrange on a plate and garnish with olives or capers and sprigs of parsley.

CRISP FILO MUSHROOM PARCELS ❦

*I*rresistible morsels, these are little mushrooms wrapped up in filo pastry and cooked until crisp and golden. Eat them freshly made, on toothpicks if you are offering them as a nibble to go with cocktails, or on small plates garnished with parsley.

MAKES 24

7 ounces filo pastry   24 tiny button mushrooms
olive oil

Leave the sheets of filo pastry stacked. Cut the stack into 4-inch squares, then separate them; you need 24 squares. Brush each square with olive oil and place a tiny mushroom in the center. Fold the filo around the mushroom to make a parcel. Brush the outside with more olive oil.

Bake on a metal baking sheet in a preheated 400°F oven until golden crisp, about 20 minutes. Let cool at least 5 minutes before serving.

MUSHROOM TRIANGLES

*C*risp golden-brown parcels of filo pastry contain a creamy mushroom mixture that is flavored with garlic and fresh herbs.

MAKES 4

2 tbsp olive oil   ¼ cup cornstarch
1 cup chopped shallots   2 tbsp chopped fresh basil or
2-3 cloves garlic, minced   tarragon
½ pound mushrooms, sliced   sea salt and freshly ground
(about 3 ½ cups)   black pepper
2 tbsp dry white wine   4 sheets filo pastry
1 cup heavy cream   melted butter
1 cup milk   beaten egg for glazing

Heat the oil in a large saucepan and cook the shallots gently, covered, until soft, about 5 minutes. Add the garlic and mushrooms and cook uncovered 8–10 minutes longer, stirring occasionally. Add the wine and boil until it has evaporated, then stir in the cream. Bring to a boil and boil gently for 5 minutes.

Mix the milk with the cornstarch, then add to the pan and bring back to a boil, stirring well. The mixture should be very thick. Remove from the heat and stir in the basil or tarragon. Season to taste. Let cool.

Cut one sheet of filo in half lengthwise. Brush one filo strip with melted butter and set the other strip on top. Brush with butter again. Spoon one-quarter of the mushroom mixture onto one end of the layered filo strip. Bring one corner up over the filling and press it onto the opposite side of the strip, to make a diagonal fold. Press the edges together to seal. Flip this triangle shape up on the pastry strip. Continue flipping the triangle over and over, to the end of the strip. Fill and shape three more triangles in the same way.

Put the mushroom triangles on a baking sheet and brush them with beaten egg. Bake in a preheated 425°F oven until the pastry is crisp and golden brown, 8–10 minutes. Serve warm.

OPPOSITE: Crisp Filo Mushroom Parcels, served with Light Tomato Sauce (see page 151) and Sour Cream Onion Dip (see page 156)

JUICES

*V*egetable and fruit juices are not only delicious, they are renowned for their health-giving qualities. They are full of flavor as well as being packed with minerals and vitamins. These nutrients are absorbed very quickly into the body, and have a fast revitalizing effect. Alternative-medicine practitioners use them in the treatment of numerous specific ailments and diseases.

Regular intake of vegetable and fruit juices maintains vitality and general good health. They are best drunk as fresh as possible, although you can keep them for several hours in an airtight jar in the refrigerator. For best results, use an electric juicer – juicing by hand to produce more than a small glassful can be exhausting, and is impossible for most vegetables.

FRUIT JUICES ♥

*T*hese are deliciously refreshing at any time of year, and always best when the fruit is in full season. Try squeezed juices: orange, grapefruit, lemon and tangerine; or juices extracted in an electric juicer: apple, apricot, blackberry, blueberry, blackcurrant, grape, kiwi, mango, melon, pineapple, pear, peach, papaya, plum, raspberry, strawberry. You can mash banana and add it to the above.

Some aromatic mixtures are:

banana and peach	banana and berries
banana and apple	pear and apple
mango and orange	peach and apricot
pineapple and peach	grape and apple

Or, you can mix fruit and vegetable juices. The variety is endless, and you will enjoy trying out all the different combinations possible as the seasons turn. Some suggested combinations are:

carrot and apple	apple and celery
carrot and orange	cucumber and apple
celery and pineapple	cucumber and peach

VEGETABLE JUICES ♥

*C*arrot, tomato, and cucumber juices are very pleasant drunk straight. If you prefer, you can mix them with a small amount of strong-tasting juices such as spinach, lettuce, cabbage, celery, beet, parsley or watercress, which are too strong to drink on their own in any quantity.

You can make excellent "juice cocktails." Serve them on ice garnished with fresh herbs. Here are some delicious combinations:
carrot, beet, and cucumber
carrot and cucumber
cabbage, celery, and tomato
tomato and alfalfa sprouts
carrot, celery, tomato, bell pepper, spinach, and
   beet with a touch of parsley and watercress

OPPOSITE: (left to right) In the bottles: beet, orange; in the box, back row: red grape and apple, carrot, pink grapefruit; front row: peach, cucumber and apple, papaya; front of picture: fresh tomato

CHAPTER THREE

Main Courses

Among the delights of cooking with vegetables is
the huge variety of dishes that you can make.
When it comes to the main part of the meal, though,
some people still feel that a vegetarian dish is not as
substantial as one that contains meat. So to satisfy that
need, which also applies to people who are trying to give
up meat and finding that they miss it, food technology
has come up with some delicious vegetable-based
alternatives.

The quality of T.V.P., or textured vegetable protein, has
come a long, long way since the early days when it was,
frankly, almost inedible. Today's T.V.P. is excellent, and is
available as mince (similar to ground meat), as chunks,
sausages, and burgers. It is highly nutritious, too,
containing 32 g protein per 100 g. For notes on how to
use meat substitutes, see page 186.

T.V.P. can be added to most of the recipes in this
chapter. Or, if you don't like T.V.P., you can omit it from
the recipes here that use it, adding more vegetables as
an alternative. In the same way, you can leave out onions
and celery if you don't like them, increasing other
vegetables that you do like. Interpret
the recipes to suit your tastes and
those of your family.

CHILI NON CARNE ⌄

The classic chili – made with vegetarian mince chunks instead of meat! It can be served either with rice or with baked potatoes, and a tossed salad of your choice. Mexican corn bread (see page 34) is another delicious accompaniment.

FOR 4

2 tbsp olive oil	1 can (16 ounces) crushed tomatoes
1 large onion, finely sliced	
2 cloves garlic, minced	1 can (16 ounces) red kidney beans, drained
2 tsp chili powder or more to taste	
	1-2 canned mild green chiles, drained and chopped (optional)
½ pound vegetarian mince	
2 cups vegetable stock	sea salt

Heat the oil and sauté the onion for 3–4 minutes, then add the garlic, chili powder and mince and stir until well mixed. Brown 5 minutes, stirring. Add the stock and the tomatoes with their juice, then let simmer gently, covered, for 20 minutes.

Add the kidney beans and the optional green chiles and simmer 15 minutes longer.

Season to taste with a little salt if necessary, and let stand 10 minutes before serving so the flavors can develop.

TASTY BEANBURGERS

So quick and easy to prepare, these beanburgers make a scrumptious lunch. Add a little chopped salad or a slice of cheese inside each bun, and serve with broiled tomatoes and the green bean salad on page 141.

MAKES 4

2 tbsp olive oil plus more for frying burgers	1 ⅓ cups fresh bread crumbs
	1 free-range egg
1 onion, finely chopped	¼ tsp chili powder or more to taste
2 cloves garlic, finely sliced	
1 tsp cumin seeds (optional)	sea salt and freshly ground black pepper
2 tbsp chopped parsley	
1 can (16 ounces) black-eyed peas or cannellini beans, drained	warm hamburger buns for serving

Heat the oil and soften the onion and garlic, covered, for 5–6 minutes. Add the cumin seeds and cook 3 minutes longer. Off the heat, stir in the parsley and the beans. Mash until smooth, or purée in a food processor. Stir in the bread crumbs and then the egg, mixing thoroughly. Season to taste with chili powder, salt, and pepper.

Shape into four burgers and shallow-fry in hot olive oil until lightly browned, 3–4 minutes on each side. Serve inside warm hamburger buns, with a little chopped salad or a slice of cheese.

STIR-FRY OF SPRING VEGETABLES WITH NOODLES ✿

A quick supper dish with fresh flavors and appetizing spicing. Stir-fries make healthy, nutritious meals that you can vary widely, using different vegetables and herbs in season. Vegans can make this with plain noodles.

FOR 4

3 green onions, finely sliced	*3 tbsp soy sauce*
½-inch piece fresh gingerroot, peeled and finely grated	*1 tbsp bean sauce*
	2 tbsp dark sesame oil
2 cloves garlic, finely sliced	*½ pound Chinese egg noodles, cooked and drained (or you can use rice noodles)*
3 ounces thin green beans	
6 ounces baby corn	
1 pound zucchini	*6 ounces firm tofu, cut in cubes and browned in olive oil (optional)*
½ pound leeks	
½ pound young carrots	
2 tbsp vegetable oil	*2 tbsp sesame seeds*

Prepare the green onions, ginger, and garlic. Trim all the vegetables and slice them finely, diagonally.

Heat the oil in a wok and add all the prepared vegetables plus the green onions, ginger, and garlic. Stir-fry briskly together for 4–5 minutes. Add the soy sauce and bean sauce and stir-fry 2 minutes longer, then cover and cook gently until all the vegetables are tender but still slightly crisp, about 5 minutes.

Add the dark sesame oil. Add the cooked noodles and the browned tofu, if using, and toss to mix with the vegetables. Sprinkle with the sesame seeds, and serve immediately.

Stir-frying

A quick, easy, and tasty way of cooking vegetables, this is best done in a wok, but failing that you can use a large frying pan. Cut your fresh vegetables into bite-size pieces, diagonally if you prefer; in some cases they need to be shredded or sliced finely and this can be done very quickly in the food processor.

Heat a very little oil in your wok or pan and smear it over the surface. Peanut oil is excellent for stir-frying because it is tasteless and doesn't burn easily. Olive oil is also good, but don't use your best quality for this — leave that for salad dressings. Get the oil — and the pan — really hot before you toss in the vegetables, letting the heat sear them as you stir them in the pan. When they are evenly heated through and beginning to cook, turn the heat down a little, and stir and toss constantly until they are tender but still crisp. At this point add other seasonings recommended in the recipe. In some cases you then turn the heat right down, cover with a lid, and let the vegetables steam to a finish.

Always serve stir-fried vegetables as soon as possible after cooking as they are at their best crisp and hot from the pan.

OPPOSITE: Stir-fry of Spring Vegetables with Noodles

BEST VEGETABLE PAELLA ♥

his great classic recipe from Spain is an eye-catching dish for special occasions. The traditional fish is replaced by mushrooms, artichoke hearts, snow peas, and water chestnuts. The subtle flavor of saffron permeates the dish and gives it its lovely golden color. Serve with a watercress salad (see page 136) and fresh, warm bread.

FOR 4-6

2 tbsp margarine

2 tbsp vegetable oil

1 large mild onion, chopped

2 cups long-grain rice

3 ¾ cups vegetable stock

⅛ tsp saffron strands, soaked in a little stock

4 cloves garlic, chopped

1 cup frozen green peas, thawed

2 canned pimientos, chopped, or 1 large fresh red bell pepper, peeled and chopped

6 ounces button mushrooms, quartered

4 large tomatoes, peeled and chopped (fresh or canned)

½ pound cooked or canned artichoke bottoms or hearts, halved

6 ounces snow peas, steamed and sliced diagonally

½ cup sliced canned water chestnuts

sea salt and freshly ground black pepper

grated cheese for serving

Heat the margarine and oil in a large pan or wok. Add the chopped onion and cook over gentle heat until soft and translucent, about 10 minutes. Add the rice and cook over medium heat, stirring constantly, for a couple of minutes. Then begin to add the stock, a little at a time, and simmer until each addition is absorbed. After about 10 minutes, add the saffron and the garlic. Continue cooking for 5 minutes or so or until the rice is tender. Then stir in the rest of the ingredients and stir until heated through. Check the seasoning.

Serve as soon as possible, with grated cheese.

Skinning Peppers

Cut peppers into quarters and seed. Cut each quarter into two or three strips and place skin-side up under a hot grill. Grill for 5–6 minutes or until the skin has blistered and blackened. Remove, place in a brown paper bag, and cool. The skin will peel off easily.

Skinning Tomatoes

Put tomatoes into a large bowl and cover with boiling water. Leave to stand for about 2 minutes. Lift out one by one and pierce the skin with a sharp knife; the skin will peel off easily.

OPPOSITE: Best Vegetable Paella

NOODLE BAKE

An easy to make and unusual version of macaroni and cheese, this nutritious bake contains cottage and cheddar cheeses, milk, and sour cream, and is seasoned with fresh herbs. Serve with green vegetables cooked tender-crisp.

FOR 4

½ pound egg noodles	1½ tbsp chopped mixed fresh herbs of your choice
1¼ cups sour cream	
¾ cup cottage cheese	1 tbsp chopped chives
1¼ cups grated cheddar cheese	sea salt and freshly ground black pepper
½ cup skim or soy milk	

Cook the noodles in boiling water, then drain and rinse under cold water. Mix together the sour cream, cottage cheese, and 1 cup of the cheddar and stir in the milk. Add the herbs and season to taste. Mix thoroughly into the noodles.

Grease an 8-inch diameter soufflé dish or other deep baking dish. Tip the noodle mixture into it and sprinkle the remaining cheddar cheese on top. Bake in a preheated 350°F oven for 20–25 minutes. Serve hot.

> *Noodles*
>
> Noodles are made from a simple paste of flour (usually wheat flour) and water, sometimes some oil, and a little salt. Egg noodles have egg in the original paste and are therefore a slightly richer version of noodle.

BAKED CORN PUDDING

You can enjoy this savory pudding hot or warm. Adding canned mild chilies is a delicious touch. The golden color of all that corn makes a beautiful dish to look at, too!

FOR 3–4

3 tbsp margarine	1 can (16 ounces) whole kernel corn, drained
1 medium onion, finely chopped	
	½ cup chopped canned mild green chiles (optional)
1 large clove garlic, minced	
3 tbsp flour	½ tsp sea salt
1 tsp ground mace (optional)	freshly ground black pepper
⅔ cup skim or soy milk	3 free-range eggs, beaten

Melt the margarine in a saucepan and cook the onion and garlic over a gentle heat, covered with a lid, until quite soft, about 10 minutes. Stir from time to time. Sift the flour with the mace, if using, then stir into the softened vegetables. Gradually add the milk, stirring all the time. When smoothly blended, cook gently 1 minute more.

Remove from the heat and stir in the corn, the optional chiles, the salt, and pepper to taste. Stir in the beaten eggs.

Pour into a greased 8- or 9-inch diameter soufflé dish or other deep baking dish. Bake in a preheated 350°F oven until the center of the pudding is just set, 40–45 minutes.

VEGETABLE HOTCH-POTCH ✦

*L*ong, slow cooking brings out all the flavors of the ingredients in this hotch-potch to perfection and fills the kitchen with wonderful appetizing smells.

FOR 6

1 pound vegetarian steak chunks

vegetable oil

¾ pound onions, sliced

1 pound potatoes, peeled and sliced

1 can (16 ounces) butter or lima beans, drained (or equivalent cooked dried, see page 185)

1 tbsp dried mixed herbs of your choice

sea salt and freshly ground black pepper

4-5 cups vegetable stock

Brown the steak chunks in a little oil. Layer the steak chunks, onions, potatoes, and butter beans in a casserole. Season as you go with the herbs, lots of pepper, and a little salt. Pour enough stock into the casserole just to cover the top layer.

Cover the casserole tightly with a lid and cook in a preheated 400°F oven for 30 minutes. Turn the temperature down to 325°F and cook for another 30 minutes. Let cool a little before serving, with steamed vegetables such as cauliflower, broccoli, or leeks.

BELOW: Vegetable Hotch-potch

MEATLESS LOAF

The art of the meatless loaf is to tailor it to your taste – add your family's favorite spices or herbs, plus chopped, cooked vegetables of your choice to ring the changes. Green peas, celery, leeks, broccoli, and corn will all give interesting tastes and textures to the basic loaf here. Instead of the stock, you can add a 16-ounce can of crushed tomatoes with their juices, to make a very moist and tomatoey-tasting loaf.

Mix all the ingredients together in a large bowl, or blend in a food processor. Pack into a well-greased 9- x 5-inch loaf pan and bake in a preheated 350°F oven until crisp on top and set, about 1 hour. Let cool in the pan at least 15 minutes before unmolding. If you are cooking ahead of time, loosen the edges after 15 minutes, and unmold when cold.

Serve with rich tomato sauce (see page 151) and Yorkshire puddings (see opposite).

FOR 6

4 ⅓ cups vegetarian mince	2 cups vegetable stock
1 onion, chopped and softened in a little olive oil	1 tbsp chopped mixed fresh thyme and sage
4-6 ounces button mushrooms, sliced (1 ¾-2 ½ cups)	1-2 tsp ground mace, or 1 tsp chili powder or ground allspice (optional)
1⅓ cups fresh bread crumbs	2 tbsp tomato paste
2 free-range eggs, beaten well	freshly ground black pepper

Dealing with Onions

Peeling pungent onions can make your eyes tear, so work near the cold water faucet and rinse your hands frequently – it will reduce the effect of the onions.

Softening onions in oil or margarine, which is such a basic step in so many recipes, is best done by first tossing the sliced or chopped onions in the oil or fat over moderate heat until well coated and then turning the heat down very low, covering the pan with a lid and leaving the onions to cook very gently for 10–12 minutes. They become very soft and sweet because this process steams them rather than browns them. Stir just once or twice during the cooking.

Browning onions is done over higher heat – and they taste much stronger than onions softened by the method above.

Main Courses

YORKSHIRE PUDDINGS

*Y*orkshire puddings are very simple to make in the blender – in a matter of seconds your batter is ready. Always leave the batter to stand in a cool place, or the refrigerator, for an hour before using so that the flour can absorb the liquids fully.

MAKES 12

1⅔ cups all-purpose flour	*2½ cups skim or soy milk*
¼ tsp sea salt	*vegetable oil for the pans*
2 free-range eggs	

Put the ingredients in a blender and blend until the batter is smooth. Let stand 1 hour.

Pour a little oil into each of 12 muffin or popover pans and heat in a preheated 425°F oven for 3–4 minutes. Spoon the batter into the pans and return to the oven. Bake 10 minutes, then turn the temperature down to 375°F and bake until risen and golden brown, about 15 minutes longer. Serve as soon as possible.

SAUSAGES BAKED IN BATTER

*C*risp, tasty sausages baked inside a cloud of light, golden batter makes popular family food. Here is the meatless version of a classic British recipe called Toad in the Hole.

FOR 4–6

1 ⅔ cups all-purpose flour	*6 large vegetarian sausage links*
¼ tsp sea salt	
2 free-range eggs	*¼ cup vegetable oil, plus extra for browning the sausages*
2 ½ cups skim or soy milk	

Sift the flour with the salt and put into a blender with the eggs and milk. Blend to a smooth batter, and let stand 1 hour in the refrigerator.

Lightly brown the vegetarian sausages in a skillet.

Heat the ¼ cup vegetable oil in a 10-inch square baking pan in a preheated 425°F oven for 5 minutes. Place the sausages in the oil and pour the batter over the top. Return to the oven and bake 15 minutes, then turn the temperature down to 375°F and bake until the batter is cooked through and golden, about 20 minutes longer.

Serve with tomato sauce (see page 151) or salsa (see page 152).

NEXT SPREAD: The main dishes for a satisfying Sunday lunch here are Meatless Loaf and Yorkshire Puddings, and Eggplant and Herb Casserole, served with Potato and Cabbage Mash (see page 106), gravy (see page 155) and carrots

63

EGGPLANT AND HERB CASSEROLE

I made this recipe when I was a young girl, and recently cooked it for Pierre Franey of the New York Times on his Great Cooks TV series. It is best with a tossed salad, such as the potato and romaine on page 130, and either plain pasta or fresh bread, and goes down well with a glass of red wine.

FOR 8

3 ½ pounds ripe plum tomatoes, peeled (see page 59), or 2 cans (28 ounces each) plum tomatoes, drained	*1 tbsp each chopped fresh oregano, basil, and thyme*
½ cup olive oil	*2 pounds eggplants, sliced diagonally ¼-inch thick*
1 large onion, chopped	*flour*
2 tbsp chopped garlic	*sea salt and freshly ground black pepper*
1 can (6 ounces) tomato paste	*½ pound mozzarella cheese, sliced*

Chop the fresh or canned tomatoes in small cubes. Heat 1 tbsp of the olive oil in a saucepan and sauté the onion and garlic, stirring, for 1 minute. Add the chopped tomatoes and the tomato paste, and then the herbs. Stir well and bring to a simmer. Cover and cook over very low heat for 30 minutes.

Meanwhile, dredge the slices of eggplant in flour and sauté them in the rest of the olive oil in a large pan over medium heat until lightly browned on both sides.

Season the tomato sauce. Pour a layer of tomato sauce over the bottom of a baking dish and cover with a layer of eggplant slices. Continue making layers, finishing with eggplant. Arrange the sliced mozzarella over the top. Bake in a preheated 350°F oven until golden brown, about 1 hour.

COTTAGE CRUNCH CASSEROLE

This layered casserole is special enough to be the main dish for Thanksgiving dinner, or for other holiday or special occasions. Serve with the cheese and parsley sauce on page 155 and lots of roasted vegetables. Cranberry sauce will be welcome, too.

FOR 8

4 ¹⁄₃ cups vegetarian mince

2 free-range eggs, beaten well

2 cups water

½ pound leeks, chopped and cooked in boiling water for 10 minutes

6 ounces mushrooms, sliced (about 2 ½ cups)

½ cup chopped walnuts

1 tsp each ground mace and allspice, or 1-2 tsp curry powder (optional)

few drops of hot pepper sauce (optional)

¾ pound zucchini, steamed and sliced

6 ounces snow peas, steamed

4 sun-dried tomatoes packed in oil, finely chopped

¼ cup chopped mixed fresh herbs, e.g. parsley, fennel, cilantro, marjoram, tarragon

¼ pound mozzarella cheese, sliced

¾ cup shredded cheddar cheese

Mix the vegetarian mince with the beaten eggs and stir in the water. Let soak 30 minutes, then purée in the blender until fairly smooth. Add the prepared leeks, mushrooms, and walnuts and season with the optional spices and hot pepper sauce. You won't need salt because the mince is sufficiently salty.

Grease a large baking dish. Spread half of the mince mixture on the bottom. Layer the sliced zucchini, snow peas, tomatoes, herbs, and mozzarella over the top, and cover with the rest of the mince mixture. Sprinkle the shredded cheese over the top. Bake in a preheated 350°F oven for 1 hour.

Fresh and Home-dried Herbs

When herbs are in season – from late spring through summer – they can be used to impart wonderful flavors and fragrances to food. Fresh herbs make a distinct difference to cooked dishes, and they are delicious in salads. When fresh herbs are out of season or unavailable, dried herbs are an excellent substitute for fresh in soups, casseroles and meatless dishes.

If you grow your own herbs you can dry them quite successfully yourself. Pick them in the morning when they are at the height of their fragrance. You can then either lay them on paper in a warm place to dry out, or tie them into small bunches and hang them in a warm, dry place with plenty of air circulating around them. When brittle – after several days – strip them off their stalks and store in dark jars out of direct sunlight.

STUFFED BELL PEPPERS ∨

This dish is inspired by the cooking of the Middle East, where stuffed vegetables of all kinds play an important part. You can make the stuffing with vegetarian mince or without, adding another ⅓ cup rice in its place if you prefer.

MAKES 6

3 large bell peppers	*3 tbsp chopped parsley*
1 large onion, finely chopped	*1 tsp each ground cumin and allspice (optional)*
2 tbsp olive oil	
1 clove garlic, minced (optional)	*½ tsp chili powder (optional)*
	1 cup vegetarian mince
½ pound tomatoes, peeled (see page 59) and chopped	*½ cup long-grain rice, cooked (see page 96)*
3 sun-dried tomatoes packed in oil, chopped (optional)	*⅔ cup pine nuts*

Halve each pepper and scoop out the seeds.

Soften the onion in the oil for 7–8 minutes over low heat, covered with a lid. Add the garlic, if using, for the last 2–3 minutes. When soft, add the tomatoes, the optional sun-dried tomatoes, and the parsley and stir well. Then add the spices if using and cook gently for a minute longer. Stir in the rest of the ingredients.

Pack the mixture into the pepper halves. Place in a greased baking dish. Pour in hot water to cover the bottom of the dish, cover with foil, and bake in a preheated 375°F oven for 30 minutes. Remove the foil and bake 15 minutes longer.

QUICK MEATLESS STROGANOFF

This is sensational: a great classic recipe adapted for people who prefer to eat a meatless diet. It is lovely with noodles or rice. An amazing dish with wonderful flavors – lighter and even more epicurean than the original!

FOR 4–6

4 tbsp margarine	*2 tbsp olive oil*
2 onions, sliced	*½ pound vegetarian steak chunks*
2 tbsp flour	
⅔ cup vegetable stock	*1¼ cups sour cream*
1¼ cups white wine	*freshly ground black pepper*
½ pound small mushrooms, cut in half	*chopped parsley for garnish*

Heat the margarine in a saucepan and cook the onions, covered, until soft. Add the flour, mixing it in well, then stir in the stock followed by the white wine. Add the mushrooms. Simmer gently, uncovered, for about 5 minutes, stirring occasionally.

Meanwhile, heat the oil and toss the steak chunks until browned all over. Mix them into the mushroom sauce. Stir in the sour cream, season generously with pepper, and cook very gently (without boiling) for 6–8 minutes. Serve sprinkled with chopped parsley

OPPOSITE: Stuffed Bell Peppers

MUSHROOM MOUSSAKA

A great dish for a dinner party, served with your favorite rice dish and a seasonal salad, such as the arugula and spinach salad on page 129. Add a basket of crusty bread and a bottle of retsina – and transport yourselves to the Mediterranean!

FOR 6

2 medium eggplants, sliced

5 tbsp olive oil

sea salt and freshly ground black pepper

1 large onion, sliced

1 clove garlic, minced

1½ pounds open-cup mushrooms, or wild mushrooms if available, sliced (about 10 cups)

1 can (16 ounces) tomatoes, drained and chopped, or 6 large fresh tomatoes, peeled (see page 59) and chopped

1 tbsp balsamic vinegar or fresh lemon juice

⅓ cup chopped parsley

1 tbsp each chopped fresh marjoram and thyme

1¼ pounds potatoes, peeled and boiled "al dente," then sliced

2 cups vegetarian mince browned in 1 tbsp vegetable oil (optional)

¼ cup ricotta cheese

2 cups béchamel sauce (see page 155)

3 tbsp shredded cheddar cheese

Brush the eggplant slices with 3 tbsp of the olive oil and sprinkle them with salt. Arrange in a single layer on a baking sheet and bake in a preheated 350°F oven for 15 minutes.

In a large pan, heat the rest of the olive oil and soften the onion and garlic, covered, for 10 minutes over medium-low heat. Stir occasionally. Then add the mushrooms and toss thoroughly. Cook, half covered with a lid, until they have softened. Add the chopped tomatoes, vinegar or lemon juice, parsley, marjoram, and thyme and mix well. Season to taste with sea salt and freshly ground black pepper. Simmer 5 minutes.

Make a layer of the potato slices in the bottom of a shallow baking dish. Continue making layers with the eggplant, mushroom mixture, remaining potatoes, and optional vegetarian mince. Finish with eggplant. Press down. Stir the ricotta into the béchamel until well blended and spoon evenly over the surface. Sprinkle with the shredded cheese. Bake in a preheated 350°F oven for 40–45 minutes.

Wild Mushrooms

There is a wonderful choice of wild mushrooms if you wish to harvest your own from the woods and fields. Chanterelles, puffballs, morels, boletus and field mushrooms all have unique flavours which are superb in a variety of recipes. Always take a good field guide with you, however, to make sure you have picked the right mushroom. A few wild mushrooms are poisonous.

Failing the mushroom-hike, try the Chinese mushrooms commonly sold in supermarkets – shiitake and oyster mushrooms have their own distinctive and delicate flavour.

CRISPY MUSHROOM LAYERS ♥

*L*ayers of a crisp crumb and nut mixture surround a garlicky mushroom filling. Delicious! Serve with baked potatoes and a salad such as the special arugula salad on page 129.

FOR 4–6

4 cups whole-wheat bread crumbs	*1 can (16 ounces) tomatoes, drained and chopped, or ¾ pound fresh tomatoes, peeled (see page 59) and chopped*
1 cup finely chopped mixed nuts	
6 tbsp margarine	*2 cloves garlic, minced*
1 large onion, finely chopped	*2 tsp dried mixed herbs of your choice*
10 ounces open-cup mushrooms, sliced (about 4 cups)	*sea salt and freshly ground black pepper*

Mix the crumbs and nuts together. Melt 4 tbsp of the margarine and fry this mixture until golden. Set aside.

Melt the rest of the margarine in another pan, add the onion, cover, and cook over a low heat until softened, 5–8 minutes. Add the sliced mushrooms and toss thoroughly, then cover the pan again and cook gently 3–4 minutes. Add the tomatoes, garlic, and herbs and stir well. Season to taste.

Make a layer of half of the bread-crumb mixture on the bottom of a baking dish and place the mushroom filling on top. Finish with a layer of the remaining crumb mixture. Bake in a preheated 375°F oven until crisp and golden, about 30 minutes. Serve piping hot.

MEATLESS MEATBALLS WITH SAUCES

*T*hese are crisp on the outside and fine and smooth inside, and are quite delicious with a variety of different sauces such as roasted red pepper sauce (see page 149), the chili sauce on page 152, the tarragon and mustard sauce on page 149 or the sauce of wild mushrooms (page 154). Serve with a potato dish of your choice, or shape the mixture into vegetarian burgers.

MAKES 12

2 cups vegetarian mince	*2 free-range eggs, beaten*
1 onion, finely chopped	*sea salt and freshly ground black pepper*
¼ cup shredded cheddar cheese	*ground mace and allspice (optional)*
2 tbsp chopped mixed fresh mixed herbs of your choice, or ½ tbsp dried mixed herbs	*flour*
	vegetable oil
⅔ cup fresh bread crumbs	

Mix the vegetarian mince with the onion, cheese, herbs, bread crumbs, and eggs in the blender. Blend until the mixture is smooth and quite fine. Season to taste with salt and pepper and add a little optional spice to taste. At this point you can also add grated zucchini, shredded leek, or some cooked spinach, if desired.

Form into small meatballs and roll in flour to coat lightly. Fry in hot shallow vegetable oil over medium heat until nicely browned all over. Drain on paper towels and serve hot.

OPPOSITE: Meatless Meatballs with Chili Sauce and Tarragon and Mustard Sauce

SIMPLE VEGETABLE CURRY ♥

*Y*ou can vary the vegetables endlessly for this "dry" curry, according to season and your choice – leeks, cauliflower, and broccoli are all delicious spiced, as are green beans, snow peas, or corn. You can also add browned vegetarian steak chunks and let them heat through in the sauce for the last 10 minutes of cooking.

FOR 3–4

1 large onion, sliced	1 large potato, scrubbed and diced
2 cloves garlic, sliced	
2 tbsp olive oil	½ pound carrots, sliced (about 2 cups)
2 tbsp Madras curry paste or to taste	½ pound zucchini, diced (about 2 cups)
1 ¼ cups frozen green peas, thawed	¼ pound mushrooms, sliced (about 1½ cups)

Soften the onion and garlic gently in the oil over low heat, covered with a lid, for 10 minutes. Stir occasionally. When they are soft, add the curry paste and stir for a few moments, then add the prepared vegetables. Toss until they are all well coated with the curried onion mixture. Cover tightly with a lid and cook over very low heat until the vegetables are tender, 30–40 minutes. (This steams the vegetables, bringing out all their flavors, and their juices are exuded so you don't need to add stock.)

When they are cooked, remove from the heat and let stand until you are ready to eat – this dish improves with waiting. Serve with plain or fried rice, and naan bread.

EASY CAULIFLOWER DHAL ♥

A lovely "dry" dhal with gentle spicing, this Indian dish goes beautifully with the Chinese egg-fried rice on page 94, some cucumber raita, and a crisp green salad.

FOR 4–6

1 ¼ cups green lentils, soaked 1-2 hours	3 cloves garlic, minced
1 large onion, sliced	2 tbsp olive oil
2-inch piece fresh gingerroot, bruised	2 tsp each ground turmeric, coriander, and cumin or to taste
1½ tbsp chopped parsley	1 head cauliflower, cut in florets and cooked
1 fresh hot green chile pepper	sea salt

Drain the lentils and put them in a saucepan with the onion, piece of gingerroot, parsley, and whole chile pepper. Cover with water, bring to a boil, and simmer 30 minutes.

Meanwhile, cook the garlic gently in the oil until soft, 3–4 minutes, then stir in the ground spices. Toss the cauliflower florets in the spiced mixture until well coated, and season to taste with sea salt.

Drain the lentils, remove the ginger and chile pepper, and mix thoroughly with the spiced cauliflower.

CURRIED CHICK PEAS WITH ONIONS ∨

Adeliciously spicy dish that is simple to prepare, and very nutritious. Serve spooned over plain boiled rice or the saffron rice on page 94, and with pita bread or naan.

FOR 4

2 tbsp olive oil	*2 cans (16 ounces each) chick*
2 onions, thinly sliced	*peas (garbanzo beans)*
2 cloves garlic, minced	*3 tbsp fresh lemon juice*
2 tbsp sesame seeds	*1 tsp tamari or light soy sauce*
1 tbsp curry powder or to taste	*3 tbsp chopped fresh parsley*
sea salt	*freshly cooked rice for serving*

Heat the oil in a large frying pan and cook the onion and garlic very gently, covered, until meltingly soft and golden, about 25 minutes. Stir in the sesame seeds and curry powder. Season with salt. Cook uncovered for 5 minutes, stirring occasionally.

Drain the chick peas, reserving ½ cup of the liquid. Add the chick peas to the pan with the reserved liquid and cook, stirring frequently, until the chick peas are hot and almost all the liquid has evaporated.

Stir in the lemon juice, tamari, and parsley. Serve hot, spooned over rice.

BELOW: Curried Chick Peas with Onions

SUMMER STEW WITH VEGETABLES ▾

A satisfying stew for people who don't want to eat meat but still like its texture. You can, of course, vary the vegetables – for a more exotic combination, try okra, broccoli, green beans, eggplant, and bell peppers. You can vary the spicing, too, to your choice, adding mace or chili powder, for example.

FOR 4

1 large onion, sliced	*2 heaping tbsp cornstarch, mixed with 3 tbsp water*
1 large clove garlic, sliced	
2 tbsp olive oil	*1 can (16 ounces) crushed tomatoes with juice*
1 baby turnip, cubed	
6 ounces young carrots, sliced (about 1½ cups)	*3-4 tbsp chopped fresh parsley, thyme, tarragon, or other mixed herbs*
6 ounces new potatoes, washed and diced (about 1¼ cups)	*optional spices, to taste*
6 ounces cauliflower florets (about 2 cups)	*sea salt and freshly ground pepper*
½ pound baby zucchini, sliced (about 2 cups)	*3 tbsp vegetable oil*
2 ½ cups vegetable stock	*½ pound vegetarian steak chunks*

In a large pan, soften the onion and garlic in the olive oil, covered, over low heat. Then add the prepared vegetables and brown 5–6 minutes, stirring and turning. Gradually add the stock, stirring, and bring to a boil, then stir in the cornstarch and water mixture. Add the tomatoes with their juice and stir well. Add the herbs, plus any spices that you choose. Season to taste. Turn the heat right down and cover the pan tightly. Simmer gently about 25 minutes, stirring occasionally.

Meanwhile, heat the vegetable oil in a shallow pan and brown the steak chunks all over for about 3 minutes. Stir the steak chunks into the stew, cover again, and cook gently 10 minutes longer. Check the seasoning, and it is ready to serve.

OPPOSITE: Summer Stew with Vegetables

SPINACH CRÊPES WITH MUSHROOMS

*A*lthough this takes a little time to prepare, it is well worth the work! The spinach crêpes are wrapped around a garlicky mushroom filling, and finished off in the oven with a topping of melting mozzarella. A lovely supper dish, ideal served with a sauce of your choice plus steamed vegetables and a fennel salad (page 134) or green bean salad (page 141).

FOR 4 (makes 8)

¾ cup all-purpose flour	*2 tbsp margarine*
sea salt and freshly ground black pepper	*1 ¼ pounds mushrooms, thinly sliced (about 8 cups)*
1 free-range egg, beaten	*3 large cloves garlic, minced*
1¼ cups skim or soy milk	*3 tbsp all-purpose flour*
1 cup cooked spinach (from 14 ounces fresh), thoroughly drained (squeeze in your hands to remove excess water)	*6 tbsp skim or soy milk*
	grated nutmeg
	¼ pound mozzarella cheese, diced
vegetable oil	*parsley for garnish*

Sift the flour and seasonings into a blender, add the egg and milk, and blend until smooth. Add the spinach and blend again. Thin out the batter with more milk if necessary – the consistency depends on the amount of water in the spinach.

Brush an 8-inch crêpe pan or frying pan with oil and heat it, then add 2 ladlefuls of the crêpe batter. Spread it to cover the bottom of the pan evenly. Cook the crêpe for 1 minute before turning to brown the other side. Keep it warm while you cook the remaining crêpes.

Heat the margarine in another pan and cook the mushrooms with the garlic until the juices run, 3–4 minutes. Stir in the flour to soak them up, then gradually add the milk a little at a time, stirring so that the sauce is smooth. Season to taste with salt, pepper, and nutmeg.

Fill the crêpes with the mushroom mixture, roll them up and place in a baking dish. Scatter the mozzarella over the top and bake in a preheated 350°F oven for 15 minutes. Serve hot, garnished with parsley.

OPPOSITE: Spinach Crêpes with Mushrooms, served with Green Bean Salad

LAYERED VEGETABLE TERRINE

*F*estival and party food par excellence, this beautiful three-colored loaf makes a meal for special occasions. It takes a while to make, but repays you handsomely.

FOR 6

1¼ pounds cauliflower, steamed until tender	*2 tsp ground ginger or to taste*
1¼ pounds carrots, steamed until tender	*1 tsp grated nutmeg or to taste*
¾ pound fresh spinach, cooked and thoroughly drained	*sea salt and freshly ground black pepper*
6 tbsp crème fraîche or light cream	*6 free-range eggs*
2 tbsp chopped fresh cilantro	*6 ounces large mushrooms, sliced (about 2½ cups)*
3 green onions, finely chopped	

In three separate operations, purée the cauliflower, carrots, and spinach, adding 2 tbsp crème fraîche or cream to each. Season the cauliflower with the chopped cilantro, the carrots with the green onions and ginger, and the spinach with the nutmeg. Add salt and freshly ground black pepper to all three mixtures. Stir 2 beaten eggs into each mixture.

Grease a 9 x 5-inch loaf pan. Place the cauliflower mixture on the bottom and arrange a layer of half the sliced mushrooms on top. Cover with the carrot mixture and add a layer of the remaining mushrooms. Finally, pour the spinach mixture over the top. Place the loaf pan in a roasting pan of hot water and bake in a preheated 400°F oven until a sharp knife inserted in the center comes out clean, 50–60 minutes.

Let stand at least 10–15 minutes before attempting to unmold. Run a knife around the edge of the terrine to loosen the sides, then invert onto a large plate and tap the base of the pan until the terrine comes out. Serve with a wonderful sauce of your choice (see pages 149 to 152).

OPPOSITE: Layered Vegetable Terrine, with Roasted Red Pepper Sauce (see page 149)

VEGETABLE SOUFFLÉ

Cauliflower makes a particularly good soufflé, and there are, of course, endless variations on the theme. You can substitute other cooked vegetables such as spinach (well drained), zucchini, broccoli, asparagus, mushrooms or green peas, using this master recipe. Grated cheddar or other hard cheese (¾ cup) is another option.

FOR 4

1 tbsp chopped green onion or shallot	*For the soufflé base:*
1 tbsp margarine	*4 tbsp margarine*
2 cups cooked cauliflower florets, cut small	*5 tbsp flour*
	1¼ cups hot skim or soy milk
	pinch each of cayenne pepper and grated nutmeg
	sea salt and freshly ground pepper
	4 free-range eggs, separated

Soften the green onion or shallots in the margarine, then toss in the cauliflower florets and cook gently for 2 minutes. Set aside.

To make the soufflé base, melt the margarine in a heavy saucepan and stir in the flour until smooth. Gradually add the hot milk and stir until smooth and thick. Season to taste with the spices, salt, and pepper. Simmer very gently for 3–4 minutes. Off the heat, stir in the egg yolks, mixing well. Fold in the cauliflower mixture. Beat the egg whites until very stiff, and fold carefully into the cauliflower mixture.

Spoon into a well-greased 8-or 9-inch diameter soufflé dish and put into a preheated 400°F oven. Turn the temperature down to 375°F and bake until the soufflé is well risen and golden on top, but still a little creamy in the center, 25–30 minutes. Serve immediately.

GOAT CHEESE AND DILL SOUFFLÉ

Soufflés are very quick and easy to make once you master the basics, and there are infinite variations you can try. Lovely with new potatoes and steamed zucchini.

FOR 4

4 tbsp margarine	*2 tbsp chopped fresh dill*
6 tbsp flour	*4 free-range eggs, separated*
1¼ cups hot skim or soy milk	*sea salt and freshly ground black pepper*
¼ pound soft goat cheese or feta cheese, cut in small cubes	

Melt the margarine in a small heavy saucepan and stir in the flour until smooth. Gradually add the hot milk and stir until smooth and thick. Simmer very gently for 3–4 minutes, then stir in the cheese and the dill. Off the heat, stir in the egg yolks and season with salt and pepper.

Beat the egg whites until very stiff, and fold carefully into the cheese mixture. Spoon into a well-buttered 8-inch diameter soufflé dish and bake in a preheated 400°F oven until well risen and golden on top, but still creamy in the center, 20–25 minutes. Serve immediately.

OMELETTES

An omelette is one of the simplest and quickest dishes ever. Leave it plain and serve with vegetables or a salad, or add a filling. Use fillings such as mushrooms sautéed with garlic and parsley, shredded cheddar cheese, lots of chopped fresh herbs with croutons if you like, sliced tomatoes sautéed in olive oil, boiled sliced new potatoes with chives – and so on. Improvise, using your favorite vegetables and herbs!

FOR 1

2 free-range eggs	*1 tbsp margarine, or 2 tbsp*
sea salt and freshly ground	*olive oil*
black pepper	

Beat the eggs until frothy, and season to taste. Melt the margarine, or heat the oil, in an 8-inch omelette pan or frying pan over medium heat. When extremely hot but not smoking, pour in the eggs and let them cook, moving the mixture around a little to start with. When the upper surface begins to bubble, lift the cooked edges so the uncooked egg can run underneath. When the base of the omelette is lightly browned, fold in half. Cook a little longer so that the middle sets, and then flip onto a warm plate to serve.

VARIATIONS

• Separate the eggs. Beat the whites until stiff and fold into the yolks before cooking in the hot margarine or oil.
• Instead of folding the omelette, flip it over to cook both sides evenly.
• For a filled omelette, put the filling into the center while the base of the omelette is browning, then fold it and cook a minute longer.

FILLINGS FROM AROUND THE WORLD

SPANISH OMELETTE
Sauté minced onion and celery gently in olive oil until soft. Then stir in chopped canned or fresh tomatoes and season to taste.

MEXICAN OMELETTE
Soften chopped pitted olives, mild or hot chili peppers, and tomatoes in a little oil and season with ground cumin.

FRENCH FINES HERBES OMELETTE
This famous recipe uses fresh garden herbs such as chives, parsley, tarragon, marjoram, fennel, basil, etc., all minced and tossed in a little melted butter. Add to the egg mixture before cooking.

CHINESE OMELETTE
Steam beansprouts and matchstick carrots with grated fresh gingerroot and add minced garlic, sliced green onion, and a little soy sauce. You can also add some chopped fresh cilantro to the egg mixture before cooking it. This omelette is traditionally served rolled rather than folded. Try cooking it in dark sesame oil for extra flavor.

CHAPTER FOUR

Pasta, Rice and Potatoes

Pasta, rice, and potatoes are major cornerstones of the meatless diet, providing carbohydrate balance to the vegetable ingredients as well as satisfying bulk. They are endlessly versatile, and can be used to make main meals as well as side dishes. They are cheap, too, and always available.

At one time these starch foods were thought of as "fattening," and were eaten sparingly or even avoided altogether by those trying to lose weight. But, in fact, they are not fattening – it all depends what you put on them or mix them with! Cooked thoughtfully, using light sauces, mixing them with other vegetables, and flavoring them with garlic, herbs, or spices, they are an important staple of a meatless diet.

SUMMER LASAGNE

Good any time of year, but especially good made when the tomato crop is at its height, and zucchini and basil are at their best. The cheese melts between layers of vegetables and pasta and is mouthwatering. Great served with a seasonal salad and bread.

FOR 6

2 pounds small zucchini, steamed lightly and sliced

sea salt and freshly ground black pepper

large bunch of fresh basil, chopped

½ pound cottage, ricotta, feta or soft goat cheese, sliced if necessary

½ pound lasagne, cooked until "al dente" (see page 90)

1 ¼ cups béchamel sauce (see page 155)

⅔ cup crème fraîche or light cream

½ cup shredded hard cheese

3 free-range egg yolks

For the light tomato sauce:

1 small onion, finely chopped

2 tbsp olive oil

2 tsp flour

2 pounds ripe tomatoes, peeled (see page 59) and chopped, or equivalent canned tomatoes

small bunch of fresh herbs, minced

1-inch strip of orange rind (optional)

sea salt to taste

First make the tomato sauce. Heat the oil in a saucepan, add the onion, and cook over low heat, covered, until softened, 8–10 minutes. Stir in the flour and cook gently, uncovered, for 3 minutes. Stir in the rest of the sauce ingredients. Cover the pan again and simmer 5 minutes, then remove the lid and simmer 20 minutes longer, stirring occasionally. Add a little water as necessary to prevent the sauce from sticking (the finished consistency should be quite thick). Discard the orange rind.

Moisten the bottom of a baking dish with a little tomato sauce. Make a layer of sliced zucchini and season with salt and pepper. Sprinkle some chopped basil over them. Cover with slices of cheese and moisten with a little more tomato sauce. Cover with strips of lasagne. Continue making these layers until all the ingredients are used up, ending with a layer of lasagne.

Heat the béchamel gently and stir in the crème fraîche or cream. Mix in the shredded cheese until it melts, and season to taste. Off the heat, beat in the egg yolks. Pour the sauce over the top lasagne layer and bake in a preheated 375°F oven until the topping is deep golden and set, 1–1¼ hours.

SPAGHETTI WITH OLIVE OIL AND GARLIC

This is one of my favorites – it's so easy. I use lots of garlic, which I love, and which is good for you. Serve with a Caesar salad (see page 133) or the watercress salad on page 136 and some fresh bread.

FOR 2

2-3 large cloves garlic (or more according to taste), minced	freshly grated Parmesan cheese, to taste (optional)
3 tbsp olive oil	chopped fresh herbs to taste, such as parsley, basil, and oregano
freshly ground black pepper	
6 ounces spaghetti	

Stir the minced garlic into the olive oil and add lots of freshly ground black pepper.

Cook the spaghetti until "al dente" (see page 90) and drain well. Mix the garlicky oil into the hot spaghetti, add the Parmesan and herbs, and toss thoroughly. Serve immediately.

Vegetarian Parmesan

Parmesan cheese is traditionally made using animal rennet, and is not suitable for vegetarians. However, there are now a few brands of Parmesan on the market made with vegetable agents. If you cannot find one, substitute finely grated vegetarian cheddar cheese.

PASTA SHELLS WITH LEEKS AND ZUCCHINI

Tasty and looks great, too. You can substitute your favorite pasta shapes for the shells. Serve a fresh tomato salad with some mixed salad leaves alongside.

FOR 4

2-3 tbsp olive oil	3 tbsp chopped fresh basil
3 leeks, finely sliced	sea salt and freshly ground black pepper
4 medium zucchini, finely sliced	cayenne pepper
3/4 pound pasta shells	1/3 cup thinly sliced sun-dried tomatoes packed in oil
1/4 pound soft goat cheese or feta cheese, crumbled, or cheddar cheese, grated	grated cheese for serving

Heat the olive oil in a frying pan and toss in the leeks and zucchini to coat them. Turn the heat down, cover, and cook over low heat until very soft, 10–15 minutes. Stir occasionally. At the same time, cook the pasta until "al dente" (see page 90).

Stir the crumbled goat cheese into the leeks and zucchini and cook until well amalgamated. Add the basil and season to taste with salt, pepper, and cayenne. Toss into the hot, well-drained pasta and sprinkle the sun-dried tomatoes over the top. Serve immediately, with grated cheese.

OPPOSITE: Spaghetti with Olive Oil and Garlic

TAGLIATELLE WITH MUSHROOM SAUCE

*T*he lovely flavor of tarragon goes well with the gentle creamy taste of mushrooms. This is food fit for special occasions, whether formal or informal. Serve it with the green bean salad on page 141, or a tossed leaf salad, plus some fresh bread on the side.

FOR 4

1 large onion, chopped	*squeeze of lemon juice*
2 cloves garlic, finely sliced	*sea salt and freshly ground black pepper*
2 tbsp olive oil	
1 pound mushrooms	*freshly grated nutmeg (optional)*
2 tbsp each chopped fresh parsley and tarragon	*grated cheese for serving*
1 pound tagliatelle	
1 cup crème fraîche or light cream	

Cook the chopped onion and garlic in the oil, covered, over gentle heat until softened, 8–10 minutes. Put the mushrooms in a blender or food processor and run it until they are very finely chopped (or else mince them with a knife). Add them to the pan with the herbs and cook for a further 6–8 minutes. At the same time, cook the pasta until "al dente" (see page 90).

Stir the crème fraîche or cream into the sauce and heat through gently. Add the lemon juice and season to taste with salt, pepper, and nutmeg.

Mix this sauce into the hot, well-drained tagliatelle and serve immediately, with grated cheese.

PASTA TWISTS WITH SPINACH AND NUTS

*C*rème fraîche is French sour cream. It gives a delicious, subtly tart taste to pasta sauces, and combines beautifully with the strong flavor of spinach and the crunchy texture of nuts.

FOR 4

1 tbsp olive oil	*¾ pound pasta twists*
3 green onions, chopped	*⅔ cup crème fraîche or light cream*
1-2 cloves garlic, minced	
½ pound fresh young spinach, finely chopped (about 4 cups)	*½ cup chopped walnuts or pecans*
1 tbsp chopped fresh tarragon or 1 tsp dried tarragon (optional)	*sea salt and freshly ground black pepper*
	grated cheese for serving

Heat the olive oil in a frying pan or wok and soften the green onions and garlic for 1–2 minutes. Add the chopped spinach and optional tarragon and stir-fry 3–4 minutes. At the same time cook the pasta until "al dente" (see page 90). Stir the crème fraîche and walnuts into the spinach mixture and season to taste. Heat through.

Pour the sauce over the hot, well-drained pasta and toss gently. Serve with grated cheese.

SPINACH FETTUCCINE WITH CREAMY TOMATOES AND BASIL

This is a pasta dish you can run up in next to no time. Serve with French or Italian bread and a tossed green salad or the roasted pepper salad on page 139.

FOR 3–4

1 can (16 ounces) crushed tomatoes, with juice, or 3/4 pound fresh tomatoes, peeled (see page 59) and chopped	*sea salt and freshly ground black pepper*
2 tbsp olive oil	*1¼ cups crème fraîche or light cream*
3 cloves garlic, finely sliced	*½ pound spinach fettuccine*
large bunch of fresh basil, roughly chopped	*½ cup grated cheddar cheese*

Mix the tomatoes with the olive oil, garlic, and basil, and season to taste with salt and pepper. Heat very gently so the flavors blend together, then add the crème fraîche or cream and stir until smoothly blended. Leave to warm through over the lowest possible heat.

Cook the spinach fettuccine until "al dente" (see page 90) and drain thoroughly. Toss with the sauce. Add the grated cheddar and toss again. Serve with more grated cheese.

PENNE WITH TOMATOES AND MOZZARELLA

This fresh tomato sauce takes only minutes to prepare and is best made with full-flavored, vine-ripened tomatoes. The dish goes beautifully with a crisp green salad or the shredded zucchini salad on page 141.

FOR 4

2 tbsp olive oil	*8 sun-dried tomatoes packed in oil, chopped (optional)*
¼ cup fresh basil torn in small pieces	*sea salt and freshly ground black pepper*
6 fresh tomatoes, cut in small squares	*¾ pound penne*
6 ounces mozzarella cheese, cut in small dice	

Put the oil, basil, tomatoes, mozzarella, and optional sun-dried tomatoes in a bowl. Season to taste with salt and lots of freshly ground pepper. Let stand while you prepare the pasta.

Cook the penne until it is "al dente" (see page 90) and drain well. Toss the hot pasta with the sauce and serve at once.

SPAGHETTINI WITH SUN-DRIED TOMATOES, EGGPLANT AND CHILI

Using fine spaghetti adds finesse to this recipe, but if you want to vary your pasta meals you can use Japanese buckwheat noodles (soba) for this dish. Like spaghettini they are very fine, but flat, and their flavor is gorgeous. The bite of chile in the sauce is an inspired contrast to the softness of the eggplant.

FOR 4

4 shallots, finely sliced

2 cloves garlic, finely sliced

2 tbsp olive oil

1 medium eggplant, cut in small cubes

1 tsp dried mixed herbs of your choice

½ cup sliced sun-dried tomatoes packed in oil, drained

1-2 fresh hot chile peppers (according to taste), seeded and very finely sliced, or ½ cup minced canned mild green chiles, drained

1 cup crème fraîche or light cream

¾ pound spaghettini

sea salt

grated cheese for serving

Cook the shallots and garlic in the oil, covered, until soft, 5–6 minutes. Stir in the eggplant and cook for 2–3 minutes. Add the herbs, sun-dried tomatoes, and chile peppers and stir well to mix. Turn the heat down to very low, cover again, and steam 10 minutes, stirring occasionally. Then add the crème fraîche or cream and heat through for a further 5 minutes. At the same time, cook the spaghettini until "al dente" (see below).

Purée the eggplant mixture in a blender or food processor, or mash to a paste, and season to taste with salt.

Toss the sauce into the hot, well-drained spaghettini and serve immediately, with grated cheese.

How to Cook Pasta

1. Bring water (2 quarts to each 1/2 pound of pasta) to a boil with 1 tsp olive oil in a large pot and add 1/2 tsp or more sea salt.

2. Put the pasta into the water and bring back to a boil. Simmer over a medium heat for the shortest cooking time recommended on the package. Stir from time to time. Alternatively, put the pasta into the boiling water and bring back to a boil, then remove the pot from the heat and cover with a lid. Let stand off the heat for the cooking time recommended on the package, stirring from time to time.

3. To test the pasta, lift out a piece on a long-handled fork or slotted spoon: it is done when it is tender but still firm to the bite ("al dente"). Never overcook pasta.

4. Drain it in a colander, shaking well to remove all excess water. Serve immediately.

OPPOSITE: Spaghettini with Sun-dried Tomatoes, Eggplant and Chili

WINTER LASAGNE

One of the joys of this dish is that it is so easy to prepare. It can also be made well in advance and then put into the oven when you are ready to cook it. All it needs is a Caesar salad (see page 133) and warm crusty bread.

FOR 6

¾ pound mushrooms, sliced (about 5 cups)	minced garlic to taste
5 tbsp vegetable oil	dried mixed herbs of your choice
3¼ cups vegetarian mince	½ pound lasagne, cooked until "al dente" (see page 90)
1 onion, chopped	
1 can (28 ounces) tomatoes, drained and roughly chopped, or 1 ¼ pounds fresh tomatoes, peeled (see page 59) and chopped	1 pound fresh spinach, cooked and drained well, then chopped
	2 cups béchamel sauce (see page 155)
sea salt and freshly ground black pepper	¾ cup shredded cheese
	2 free-range eggs, beaten

Sauté the mushrooms briskly in 3 tbsp of hot oil until they are lightly cooked and crisp. Set aside. Mix the vegetarian mince with the minced onion and cook in the rest of the oil until the onion softens a little, 4–5 minutes.

Cover the bottom of a baking dish with chopped tomatoes and season with salt and pepper, some minced garlic, and a sprinkling of dried mixed herbs. Cover with lasagne strips and make the next layer with the mince mixture. Season again. Spread spinach on top and then the mushrooms. Continue making layers, finishing with a layer of lasagne.

Heat the béchamel gently and stir in the shredded cheese until it melts. Remove from the heat and stir in the beaten eggs. Pour over the top of the lasagne, and bake in a preheated 375°F oven until well browned on top, about 1 hour.

SPINACH-FUSILLI BAKE

The original combination of layers in this dish – spinach, garlicky pasta, and sliced tomatoes topped with cheese – makes a memorable meal served with a Caesar salad (see page 133) and fresh whole-grain bread.

FOR 3–4

1 pound fresh spinach, steamed	10 ounces fusilli, cooked until "al dente" (see page 90)
2 cups béchamel sauce (see page 155)	2 tbsp olive oil
	2 large cloves garlic, minced
sea salt and freshly ground black pepper	5 large tomatoes, sliced
grated nutmeg	½ cup shredded cheddar cheese

When the spinach is cool enough to handle, squeeze it thoroughly dry. Mix into the béchamel and season to taste with salt, pepper, and nutmeg. Cover the bottom of a baking dish with the mixture. Toss the well-drained pasta with the olive oil and garlic and spread over the spinach layer. Arrange the tomato slices over the top, in slightly overlapping layers, and season well with salt and pepper. Sprinkle the shredded cheese over the top. Bake in a preheated 350°F oven until nicely browned, 40–45 minutes.

MACARONI SPECIAL

This version of the well-known macaroni and cheese is light and creamy, and makes wholesome, satisfying family food. With the addition of mushrooms and leeks, it is almost a meal in itself, needing only some broiled tomatoes and perhaps the cauliflower salad on page 140.

FOR 4-6

½ pound elbow macaroni	*1½ cups shredded cheddar*
2 small leeks, shredded	*cheese*
2 free-range eggs	*sea salt and freshly ground*
2½ cups skim or soy milk	*black pepper*
2 tbsp margarine, melted, or	*grated nutmeg*
olive oil	*6 ounces mushrooms, sliced*
	(about 2 ½ cups)

Put the macaroni in a large pan of boiling water with the shredded leeks and simmer 5 minutes. Drain.

Whisk the eggs with the milk and add the melted margarine or oil and the shredded cheese. Season with salt, pepper, and nutmeg.

Put the macaroni and leeks in a baking dish. Cover with the sliced mushrooms. Pour the egg mixture over the top and bake in a preheated 350°F oven until the top is browned, 35–45 minutes. Leave for 10 minutes before serving, to let it set in the center and cool a little.

RICE NOODLES WITH BROCCOLI, GINGER AND GARLIC ᵛ

The combination of ginger and garlic gives a classic Asian flavor to this quick and easy supper dish. You can buy bean sauce and dark sesame oil from Chinese grocers – they are useful standbys to have on the pantry shelf.

FOR 4

1 pound rice vermicelli	*1-inch piece fresh gingerroot,*
2 ½ pounds broccoli florets	*peeled and very finely grated*
	2-3 large cloves garlic, minced
For the sauce:	*3 tbsp bean sauce*
4 green onions, very finely	*1 tbsp soy sauce or to taste*
sliced	*6 tbsp dark sesame oil*

To make the sauce, mix all the ingredients together and let stand while you cook the broccoli and vermicelli.

Cover the rice vermicelli with cold water in a large saucepan. Bring to a boil, then remove from the heat and let soak 5 minutes. Meanwhile, steam the broccoli florets and cut them small.

Drain the vermicelli thoroughly and toss with the broccoli florets and the prepared sauce.

SIMPLE SAFFRON RICE ♥

That special saffron yellow gives added pleasure to the flavor of the spices in this rice dish, and toasted cashew nuts provide a contrasting crunch.

FOR 4

1 cup basmati rice	⅛ tsp saffron strands soaked
2 tbsp olive oil	in 2 tbsp water, drained
2 fresh hot red chile peppers,	sea salt
seeded and very finely sliced	1 cinnamon stick, bruised
(optional)	⅓ cup cashew nuts, browned
3 cardamom pods, split open	lightly under the broiler
1-2 tsp cumin seeds	
½ cup frozen green peas,	
thawed	

Rinse the rice and cook it until tender (see page 96). Meanwhile, heat the oil and toss the sliced chiles, cardamom pods, and cumin seeds until they give out their aromas, about 2 minutes.

Toss the spice mixture, peas, and saffron into the drained hot rice and season with a little salt. Place the cinnamon stick in the center and sprinkle the toasted cashew nuts over for garnish.

Saffron

It used to demand a price higher than gold — and is still an expensive spice. Saffron consists of the stamens of the saffron crocus, which have to be gathered manually, and picked out by hand. Powdered saffron is an adulterated form, merely a colored and flavored mixture. So where you can, use the tiny thread-like stamens — they are intensely strong and you need only two or three to flavor a large quantity of food.

CHINESE EGG FRIED RICE

Although this is the ideal dish to go with spring rolls or a simple stir-fry, it also makes an excellent main course in its own right. It is full of interest and color, and the strips of lightly cooked free-range egg are a delicious finishing touch.

FOR 6

1 tbsp dark sesame oil	¼ pound snow peas, sliced
2 free-range eggs, beaten	diagonally
1 tbsp vegetable oil	1-inch piece fresh gingerroot,
4 green onions, finely sliced	peeled and grated
1 yellow bell pepper, seeded	2 large cloves garlic, minced
and finely diced	1 ⅓ cups long-grain rice,
1 medium carrot, cut in fine	cooked (see page 96)
matchsticks	soy sauce
1 cup sliced canned water	paprika
chestnuts	

Heat the sesame oil in a skillet and pour in the beaten eggs. Stir a little until they set like a thin omelette, then flip over to cook the other side lightly. Turn onto a wire rack and cool. Cut in thin strips.

Heat the vegetable oil in a wok until very hot. Stir-fry (see page 56) all the vegetables with the ginger and garlic for 3 minutes, then turn the heat down and cook until they are tender but still slightly crisp, about 3 minutes longer. Stir in the rice, mixing well, and season to taste with soy sauce and paprika. Finally, fold in the egg strips and it is ready to serve. Delicious with the sweet and sour sauce on page 153.

OPPOSITE: Simple Saffron Rice (top) and Chinese Egg Fried Rice with Sweet and Sour Sauce on the side

GREEK RICE WITH LEEKS ❤

This tasty dish of chili-spiced rice simmered gently with leeks is topped with thick plain yogurt, which vegans can omit.

FOR 4

¼ cup olive oil	*¾ pound leeks, sliced*
2 medium onions, roughly chopped	*sea salt and freshly ground black pepper*
2 tsp chili powder or to taste	*thick plain yogurt for serving (optional)*
1 cup long-grain rice, rinsed	
1¼ cups vegetable stock or water	

Heat the olive oil in a medium saucepan and sauté the onions until they begin to soften, 3–4 minutes. Add the chili powder and the rice and stir well to coat the grains with oil. Pour in the vegetable stock or water, stirring, then add the sliced leeks and a little salt and pepper. Bring to a boil. Turn the heat down and simmer gently, covered with a lid, until the rice is cooked, 20–25 minutes. Check the seasoning.

Heap a tablespoon of thick yogurt if using on top of each serving.

PERSIAN CHILAU RICE ❤

An unusual way of cooking rice, this has a crunchy texture and is gently spiced.

FOR 4

1 cup basmati rice	*For garnish:*
2 tsp ground cumin or to taste	*thick plain yogurt (optional)*
sea salt	*toasted sliced almonds*
2 tbsp olive oil	
2 tbsp margarine	

Rinse the rice and par-cook in boiling salted water for 5 minutes, then drain thoroughly. Mix with the cumin and a little salt.

Heat the olive oil with half of the margarine in a heavy saucepan. Pack the rice into the pan, smooth the surface, and dot with the remaining margarine. Cover closely with foil. Cover the pan tightly with a lid and turn the heat right down. Cook over the lowest possible heat until the rice is completely tender and a golden-brown crust has formed on the base, 35–40 minutes. Check the seasoning.

Spoon into a warm serving dish so that the crunchy golden bits are mingled with the soft rice, and top with a few spoonfuls of plain yogurt, if using. Scatter toasted sliced almonds over the top and it is ready to serve.

How to Cook Rice

There is a simple ratio of 1 to 2 when cooking rice: to one cup of rice you add two cups of water.

1. Rinse rice before you cook it. Then put it into a saucepan, add the measured water, and bring to a boil.

2. Turn the heat down and cover with a lid so that the pan is sealed. Let the rice cook, covered all the time, until it has absorbed all the water. This takes 8–10 minutes for white rice, or up to 20 minutes for brown or risotto rice.

3. Add some salt if you wish and fluff up the rice with a fork.

MEXICAN RICE 'N' BEANS ⓥ

So easy to make, this is hot and tasty, an interesting alternative to baked beans – and just as nutritious. Provide hot pepper sauce for those who like their Mexican food REALLY hot!

FOR 2–3

1 can (16 ounces) red kidney or black beans, drained (or equivalent cooked dried, see page 185)	2 tsp ground cumin or to taste
	1 tsp chili powder or to taste
	1 1/4 cups vegetable stock
1 large onion, chopped	1/2 cup long-grain rice, cooked (see opposite)
2 large cloves garlic, sliced	hot pepper sauce for serving (optional)
4 tbsp margarine	
1 tbsp whole-wheat flour	

In a saucepan, mix the beans with the onion and garlic. Using a fork, mix the margarine, flour, and spices to a paste. Pour the vegetable stock over the beans, add the spice paste, and heat gently, stirring, until smoothly blended. Simmer, uncovered and stirring from time to time, until the sauce thickens like gravy, about 30 minutes.

Arrange the hot cooked rice around the edge of a shallow serving dish and pour the beans into the center. Serve at once, with hot pepper sauce.

VEGETABLE-CHILI RICE ⓥ

Speed and simplicity are the keynotes here. The spicy vegetable mixture can be cooked in the time it takes to boil the rice. This is a dish likely to be a regular favorite at any time of the year.

FOR 4

1 large clove garlic, finely sliced	1 can (16 ounces) crushed tomatoes, with juice, or 6 fresh tomatoes, peeled (see page 59) and chopped
1 large onion, finely sliced	
2 tbsp olive oil	
3 stalks celery, sliced	garam masala
1 1/4 cups frozen green peas, cooked and drained	sea salt and freshly ground black pepper
1 fresh hot chile pepper, seeded and finely sliced (to taste)	1 cup long-grain rice, cooked (see opposite)

Cook the garlic and onion in the oil over gentle heat, covered with a lid and stirring occasionally, until softened, 8–10 minutes.

Stir in the celery over medium heat, then add the peas and sliced chili pepper and mix in well. Heat through, then add the chopped tomatoes and cook 5 minutes. Season to taste with garam masala, salt, and pepper.

Stir into the hot cooked rice and it is ready to serve.

MUSHROOM RISOTTO

The delicate flavors of this risotto can be varied by adding chopped pumpkin or other vegetables. It is a delicious supper dish, perfect with a salad of mixed leaves dressed in the lemony caper vinaigrette on page 147.

FOR 4

1 pound mixed mushrooms, e.g. common, shiitake, oyster, etc., sliced

4 tbsp olive oil

2 cloves garlic, minced

2 tbsp chopped parsley

1 onion, chopped

¾ cup arborio or other risotto rice

6 cups hot vegetable stock

¾ cup grated cheese

1 tbsp minced fresh tarragon

ground mace

sea salt and freshly ground black pepper

Sauté the mushrooms briskly just a minute or so in 2 tbsp of the olive oil, adding the minced garlic and chopped parsley once the juices begin to run. Remove from the heat, cover, and set to one side.

Soften the onion in the rest of the oil over a gentle heat, covered with a lid, for 6–7 minutes. Then add the rice and stir until it is well coated with oil. Add a ladleful of the hot stock and simmer, stirring, until it has been absorbed, then add another ladleful of stock. Continue adding the stock a little at a time and simmering until the rice absorbs the liquid before adding more.

When all the stock has been added and the rice is fully cooked, stir in the cheese and tarragon. Season with mace, salt, and pepper, fold in the mushrooms with all their juices, and serve.

Types of Rice

LONG GRAIN – is the most versatile and popular of all types and comes white or brown.

SHORT GRAIN – is often used for risottos and rice puddings and is usually white. If you can find brown short-grain rice, use it to make delicious, slightly more crunchy risottos.

BROWN RICE – is the best rice in nutritional terms: the whole natural grain still with its edible husk, which makes it high in dietary fiber. It has a delicious flavor and nutty texture. Brown rice, both long-grain and short-grain, needs a little more water and longer cooking than white rice.

BASMATI – is a narrow long-grain rice variety with a fabulous flavor, great with Indian food. It comes brown or white. Grown in India and Italy.

ARBORIO – from Italy, is a plump short-grain rice with good flavor. It makes excellent risottos.

POLISHED SHORT-GRAIN RICE – is perfect for a creamy rice pudding. It goes soft and mushy when cooked because of its high starch content.

WILD RICE – is not a true rice at all, but the seed of a water grass. It is long and narrow, gray-brown in color, and nutty in flavor. Wild rice requires longer cooking than other rice – 30–40 minutes. I like to mix a handful of wild rice into many of my rice dishes.

RICE FLOUR – is a good thickening agent in sauces and stews, and can be used in baking. It is invaluable for someone with a gluten allergy.

OPPOSITE: Mushroom Risotto

VEGETARIAN MINCE AND RICE v

Serve this quick supper dish with a green vegetable such as creamed spinach purée (see page 46) or lemon green beans (see page 44) or a crunchy vegetable salad.

FOR 4

2 tbsp olive oil	1 tbsp chopped fresh parsley or other herbs
1 large onion, minced	
1½ cups vegetarian mince	1 tbsp tomato paste, or 1 cup canned crushed tomatoes
1 cup long-grain rice, cooked (see page 96)	sea salt and freshly ground black pepper

Heat the oil in a wok or frying pan and sauté the onion for 5 minutes. Add the mince and stir-fry for 5 minutes or until lightly browned. Stir in the rice, herbs, and tomato paste or tomatoes. Season to taste. Heat through, stirring.

RICE AND VEGETABLE CHEESE BAKE

Mixed vegetables spiced with turmeric, cumin, and ginger are folded into rice with cheese. The full flavor of this bake goes beautifully with the roasted pepper salad on page 139 or steamed green vegetables.

FOR 6

1 onion, sliced	sea salt and freshly ground black pepper
3 tbsp olive oil	
3 zucchini, cubed	1¼ cups brown long-grain rice, cooked (see page 96)
1 yellow bell pepper, seeded and cut in small squares	1 cup shredded cheddar cheese
1 cup whole kernel corn	2 free-range eggs, beaten
1 tsp each turmeric, ground cumin, and ground ginger or to taste	2 tbsp margarine

Soften the onion in the oil for 5 minutes over a gentle heat, covered with a lid. Stir in the other vegetables and toss to mix, then cover the pan again and cook until all the vegetables are tender, about 10 minutes. stirring from time to time. Stir in the spices and season with salt and pepper. Mix into the cooked rice with the shredded cheese, and fold in the beaten eggs.

Spread the mixture in a baking dish and dot the top with the margarine. Cover the dish with foil and bake in a preheated 350°F oven for 40–45 minutes. Let rest 10 minutes before serving, with cheese and parsley sauce (see page 155).

SHEPHERD'S PIE ❤

*N*othing can beat a good shepherd's pie. Making it with vegetarian mince is even better than the original meat version because it is lighter and less greasy. You can add other chopped vegetables to the mixture, such as zucchini, broccoli, or leeks, and vary the dish each time you make it.

FOR 4-6

1½ pounds potatoes, peeled	*2 carrots, thinly sliced*
6 tbsp margarine	*2 cups vegetarian mince*
1-2 tbsp skim or soy milk	*2 tbsp soy sauce*
sea salt and freshly ground	*1¼ cups vegetable stock*
black pepper	*ground mace, grated nutmeg,*
1 large onion, chopped	*or garam masala (optional)*

Cook the potatoes in boiling water until quite soft, about 20 minutes, then drain well and mash them with 4 tbsp of the margarine and enough skim or soy milk to make a firm but smooth consistency. Season to taste.

Melt the remaining margarine in a frying pan and add the onion and carrots. Cover with a lid and cook until soft, about 10 minutes, stirring occasionally. Add the vegetarian mince, soy sauce, and vegetable stock. Bring to a boil and simmer gently, uncovered, for 8–10 minutes. Season to taste with salt and pepper and add any spices of your choice.

Put the mince mixture into a baking dish and cover with the mashed potatoes. Bake in a preheated 400°F oven until the potato topping is well browned, about 30 minutes.

TWICE-BAKED POTATOES

A nice variation on plain baked potatoes. You can vary the vegetables you put in – chopped onions or leeks, sliced mushrooms, diced bell peppers, small broccoli florets, and corn would all be delicious.

FOR 4-6

4 large baking potatoes,	*¾ cup cooked peas*
scrubbed	*¾ cup diced cooked carrots*
1¼ cups béchamel sauce (see	
page 155)	
1 cup shredded cheddar cheese	
plus more for the tops	

Bake the potatoes in a preheated 400°F oven until tender, about 1¼ hours. Cut in half lengthwise and remove the flesh, being careful not to break the skins. Put the flesh in a bowl and set the skins aside.

Heat the béchamel gently and stir in the shredded cheese until it melts. Add to the potato flesh and mash well, then fold in the prepared vegetables. Fill the potato skins with the mixture. Cover with more shredded cheese and replace in the oven. Bake until the tops are lightly browned, 6–8 minutes.

CREAMY POTATO AND LEEK BAKE

*L*ayers of thinly sliced potatoes and leeks, with a central layer of mushrooms flavored with garlic and fresh herbs, are baked under a creamy topping with crisp crumbs.

FOR 2–3

2 large cloves garlic, minced	¾ pound leeks, sliced
2 tbsp olive oil	sea salt and freshly ground black pepper
½ pound mushrooms, sliced	grated nutmeg
2 heaping tbsp chopped fresh herbs, e.g. thyme, tarragon and parsley, or ½ tbsp dried mixed herbs of your choice, plus more for the layers	¾ cup crème fraîche or light cream
	⅓ cup skim or soy milk
	1⅓ cups fresh bread crumbs
¾ pound potatoes, peeled and thinly sliced	2 tbsp margarine

Sauté the garlic in the oil for 2 minutes, then add the mushrooms and herbs and toss together. Cover and cook gently for 5 minutes.

Layer half of the potatoes and leeks in a baking dish and season with salt, pepper, nutmeg, and a sprinkling of herbs. Spoon the mushrooms and all their juices over the top and cover with the rest of the leeks and potatoes. Spoon the crème fraîche or cream over the top and add the skim or soy milk. Cover tightly with foil and cook in a preheated 375°F oven for 1 hour.

Remove the foil. Sprinkle bread crumbs over the top, dot with margarine, and bake, uncovered, until the potatoes are tender, 25–30 minutes longer.

POTATO AND EGGPLANT CURRY ♥

A beautifully spiced potato dish for cold weather. Serve with basmati rice, some naan bread, and a shredded lettuce salad with the poppy seed dressing on page 146.

FOR 3–4

1-2 tsp chili powder	1 fresh hot green chile pepper, seeded and finely chopped
½ tsp turmeric	
2 tsp ground cumin or to taste	1 cup canned crushed tomatoes, with juice, or peeled (see page 59) and chopped fresh tomatoes
1 tsp ground coriander or to taste	
1 tsp sea salt	4 medium potatoes, boiled and cut in cubes
1 tbsp tomato paste	
¼ cup vegetable oil	6 ounces vegesteak chunks, browned in a little oil (optional)
1 pound eggplant, sliced	
1-2 tsp cumin seeds	
1-inch piece fresh gingerroot, peeled and grated	fresh cilantro leaves for garnish

Mix the spices, salt, and tomato paste with 1 tbsp of the oil in a small bowl. Spread the spice mixture over the cut sides of the eggplant slices. Cut the slices into strips.

Heat the remaining oil in a frying pan and fry the cumin seeds until they begin to pop. Add the eggplant strips and grated ginger and turn the heat down. Cover and cook for 8 minutes, stirring once or twice.

Add the chile pepper, tomatoes, and potatoes with 3–4 tbsp water and simmer, covered tightly, for 15–20 minutes, stirring from time to time.

Add the browned vegesteak chunks, if using, and mix well. Serve garnished with cilantro leaves.

OPPOSITE: Potato and Eggplant Curry

SAUTÉ OF SWEET POTATOES ⌄

Sweet potatoes are loaded with beta carotene. Boil them in the same way as ordinary potatoes, as in this recipe. You can also bake them (they don't take as long as ordinary potatoes), roast them, or make into fries to serve with sour cream.

FOR 2–3

4 medium orange- or yellow-fleshed sweet potatoes (yams), peeled	½ cup firmly packed brown sugar
3 tbsp margarine	2 tbsp chopped fresh parsley or chives
grated rind and juice of 1 orange	

Cook the sweet potatoes in boiling water until they are tender, 10–15 minutes. Drain well. Slice them or cut in cubes.

Heat the margarine in a sauté pan or skillet and add the sweet potatoes. Toss over a medium heat until the potatoes are covered with margarine, then add the orange rind and juice, the sugar, and herbs. Heat through, stirring and tossing, and serve immediately.

CRISPY POTATO SKINS ⌄

These make a very healthy snack, a good alternative to potato chips. You can serve them with the spicy chili dip on page 156 or guacamole (see page 157), or any other favorite dip or salsa.

FOR 4 AS A SNACK

4 baking potatoes, scrubbed	sea salt
sunflower or canola oil	

Bake the potatoes in a preheated 400°F oven until tender, about 1¼ hours. Alternatively, microwave them 10 minutes on full power. Let cool a little, then cut in half and carefully scoop out the flesh (you can use this for mashed potatoes or a shepherd's pie, see page 101). Cut each half skin into three wide strips and then into squares.

Heat some oil in a skillet until it is very hot – when you drop the first potato skin into the oil it should immediately start to sizzle. Cook the skins quickly on both sides until golden and crisp. Drain on paper towels to absorb excess oil, sprinkle with a little salt, and they are ready to serve.

OPPOSITE: Sauté of Sweet Potatoes (left) and Crispy Potato Skins, with Green Herb Dip (see page 157)

POTATO AND CABBAGE MASH ▾

*H*ere is a traditional country dish devised just for cold, bleak winter weather.

FOR 3-4

1 pound potatoes, freshly boiled	6 green onions, finely sliced
⅔ cup skim or soy milk	pinch of grated nutmeg
3-3½ cups chopped cooked green cabbage	sea salt and freshly ground black pepper
	melted margarine

Mash the potatoes with the milk, or blend them together in a food processor. Turn into a saucepan and reheat, stirring. Add the cabbage and green onions and mix well. Season with nutmeg, salt, and pepper. Heat through.

Put into a dish, or place piles of mash on each plate, and make a deep well in the center. Fill the well with melted margarine and eat, dipping each forkful of mash into the margarine.

GARLIC MASHED POTATOES ▾

*G*arlic lovers, this is a sensational way of eating potatoes – and garlic! It is based on a simple Spanish sauce of pounded garlic and olive oil.

FOR 3-4

4 cloves garlic	2 pounds potatoes, freshly boiled and kept warm
½ tsp sea salt	freshly ground black pepper
6 tbsp olive oil	
squeeze of lemon juice	

In a mortar, pound the garlic to a fine paste with the salt. Add the oil in a slow stream, pounding all the time so that the sauce thickens. Add the lemon juice to thin out the sauce, and season with more salt if necessary.

Mash the hot potatoes well, then gradually beat in the garlic oil with an electric mixer or whisk. Season with freshly ground pepper, and serve.

SPICY BEAN BAKED POTATOES ▾

*A*n easy lunch or supper dish, this will be very popular with both children and adults. In cold weather, serve bowls of soup too – the pumpkin soup on page 20 would be especially nice.

FOR 2

2 baking potatoes, scrubbed	1 can (16 ounces) baked beans
1 tbsp olive oil	2 tbsp curry paste or to taste
1 small onion, chopped	

Bake the potatoes in a preheated 400°F oven until tender, about 1¼ hours. Alternatively, microwave them 10 minutes on full power.

Heat the oil in a pan and sauté the onion until crisp and browned, 5–6 minutes. In another pan, heat the baked beans with the curry paste.

Cut the potatoes in half lengthwise. Cut a deep cross in the flesh of each half and top with the spiced baked beans. Sprinkle with the browned onions and serve.

FRIED POTATO CAKES ⓥ

This is a delicious way to use up leftover mashed potatoes! You can vary the recipe with sautéed mushrooms, leeks or onions, or cheese.

FOR 2-4

2 cups mashed potatoes	vegetable oil
flour	margarine
sea salt and freshly ground black pepper	

Divide the mashed potatoes in 4 or 8 equal portions and shape each into a cake with floured hands. (If the potatoes are moist you will need to mix a bit of flour into them to help bind the cakes.) Season some flour with salt and pepper and use to coat the cakes lightly.

Heat a mixture of oil and margarine in a skillet and fry the potato cakes over a medium heat until crisp and golden brown on both sides. Serve hot.

ROSTI ⓥ

Serve this as a supper dish, with a Caesar salad (see page 133), or as a side dish. A crispy crust covers tender steamed, grated potatoes.

FOR 4

2 pounds potatoes, peeled	2 tbsp olive oil
sea salt and freshly ground black pepper	2 tbsp margarine

Grate the potatoes coarsely. Press dry between sheets of paper towels and season well.

Heat the oil with the margarine in a heavy frying pan over high heat. Add the potatoes and flatten into a cake. Turn the heat down, cover tightly with a lid, and cook gently until the base of the potato cake is crusty and browned and the potatoes themselves are tender, 25–30 minutes.

To unmold, place a plate over the top of the pan and turn the pan over so that the potato cake falls out onto the plate. Serve at once.

SCALLOPED POTATOES

This simple potato dish is a classic that you can vary by using all kinds of herbs and vegetables in between the layers of potato.

FOR 3-4

1½ pounds potatoes, peeled and very thinly sliced	sea salt and paprika
6 tbsp margarine	1 tsp Dijon mustard (optional)
⅓ cup finely chopped fresh chives, green onions, or leeks	1¼ cups skim or soy milk
	light cream (optional)
⅓ cup finely diced red bell pepper (optional)	¼-½ cup shredded cheddar cheese

Make layers of the potatoes in a shallow baking dish, with tiny pieces of margarine, the chives, green onions, or leeks, and optional bell peppers between them. Sprinkle each layer with sea salt and paprika as you go. Mix the mustard with a little milk, then add to the rest of the milk, with some cream if you like. Pour this over the top of the layered potatoes and sprinkle with the cheese.

Bake in a preheated 350°F oven for 1½ hours, covered with foil for the first 30 minutes.

CHAPTER FIVE

Pastry

There is something very special about the sight of a pastry dish. It looks so appetizing – crisp, golden brown, and mouthwateringly light. Perhaps an element of surprise comes into the pleasure, too, because the pastry conceals some masterly mixture that will only be revealed on the cutting into portions. The wonderful selection of recipes in this section demonstrates just how versatile pastry is. Quiches, strudels, turnovers, pies, spring rolls, and even mille-feuilles are all to be found here – plus the most popular "pie" of all, the pizza.

Fortunately, with the manufacture of refrigerated and frozen piecrust dough, a lot of the drudgery has been taken out of cooking with pastry. Excellent brands of puff pastry and piecrust dough are available everywhere, and take only a matter of moments to roll out and cut. Make sure to examine the ingredients for animal fat such as suet, or additives. Pizza bases are easily obtainable, too.

If, however, you want to make your own pastry, there are recipes on pages 178 and 179.

Pastry

MUSHROOM FILO PIE

A dramatic pie that makes a perfect party piece, this dish is full of flavor and texture – the succulence of mushrooms, the crispness of wafer-thin filo pastry, and a hint of smooth rice. Serve with the roasted red pepper sauce on page 149 and a garlicky watercress salad (see page 136) or the special arugula salad on page 129.

FOR 4–6

2 shallots, finely sliced	2 cloves garlic, minced
3 tbsp olive oil plus extra for the pastry	¼ cup chopped parsley
	2 tbsp chopped fresh tarragon
1½ pounds mixed mushrooms, e.g. shiitake, oyster, and common, all thinly sliced in the food processor	⅓ cup crème fraîche or light cream
	½ cup basmati rice, cooked (see page 96)
	6 ounces filo pastry

Soften the shallots in 1 tbsp of the oil, then add the rest of the oil. Toss in the thinly sliced mushrooms until they are well coated with oil and beginning to heat through, then turn the heat down a little and cover with a lid. Cook gently until the mushrooms are tender but not soggy, 6–8 minutes, stirring occasionally. Add the garlic and herbs and stir well, then stir in the crème fraîche or cream off the heat. Finally mix in the cooked rice and let cool.

Oil an 8-inch shallow pan, either square or round. Layer half of the filo pastry sheets in the pan, letting the edges of the pastry hang over the side of the pan all around by several inches. Brush each layer with oil as you go along. Drain excess liquid from the mushroom mixture, then spread it in the center of the pan. Fold the pastry edges into the center. Continue making layers with the rest of the filo, brushing with oil as you go, and crumpling, creasing, or twisting up the top sheets to make a pattern. Brush the top well with more olive oil.

Bake in a preheated 400°F oven until golden, about 30 minutes. Cut in wedges to serve.

VEGETABLE STRUDEL

This sensational pastry roll encases lightly cooked vegetables that are bound together with melted cheese. For something so special it is delightfully simple to prepare, and naturally you can experiment by varying the vegetables.

FOR 4–6

3 tbsp margarine, melted	6 ounces goat cheese, feta or cheddar cheese, sliced or crumbled
3 tbsp olive oil	
ten 12- x 6-inch sheets filo pastry	sea salt and freshly ground black pepper
½ pound zucchini, steamed and sliced thinly	1 ½ tbsp chopped fresh thyme
½ pound broccoli, steamed and sliced	1 tbsp chopped fresh tarragon (optional)
¼ pound thin green beans, steamed and cut in half	1 free-range egg, beaten
	flowers or herbs for garnish

Mix the melted margarine with the olive oil. Brush 5 of the filo pastry sheets with the mixture and stack them on top of each other.

Mix the prepared vegetables together with the cheese. Season with salt and pepper and add the thyme and tarragon (if using). Take half of the mixture and spread it over the surface of the stacked pastry, leaving a 2-inch margin clear all around. Fold the short edges in, and roll up from a long side like a jelly roll. Brush the surface with beaten egg and place on a well-greased baking sheet. Repeat with the other half of the ingredients to make a second strudel.

Bake in a preheated 375°F oven until golden brown and crisp, 30–40 minutes. Let stand for a few minutes before slicing, and serve on a warmed dish garnished with flowers or herbs.

VEGETABLE SPRING ROLLS ⓥ

Spring rolls are perennial favorites and the homemade variety is unbeatable. Serve these as a first course for a special meal, or as a supper dish for friends, with Chinese egg fried rice (see page 94).

MAKES 12

2 tbsp peanut or olive oil plus more for deep-frying	¾ cup beansprouts
	4 green onions, minced
3 ½ cups finely chopped mixed vegetables, such as snow peas, green peas, broccoli, zucchini, carrots, and water chestnuts	2-inch piece fresh gingerroot, peeled and grated
	1 clove garlic, minced
	2–3 tbsp soy sauce
1 ½ cups chopped button mushrooms	24 sheets filo pastry

Heat the peanut oil and stir-fry (see page 56) all the prepared vegetables with the ginger and garlic. Stir in soy sauce to taste. Remove from the heat, cover, and let stand several minutes.

Put 2 tablespoons of the vegetable filling on a single filo sheet and roll it up, tucking in the sides to make a neat parcel. Immediately roll this roll in another sheet of filo. Repeat to make 12 spring rolls in all.

Deep-fry in hot oil (375°F), turning the spring rolls, until they are light golden all over and crisp. Drain on paper towels and serve at once.

OPPOSITE: Vegetable Strudel

CREAMY VEGETABLE PIE

The joy of this pie is that you can make it across the seasons, choosing your favorite vegetables. Spring, summer, or winter, it makes a mouthwatering meal, served with noodles and the fennel salad on page 134.

FOR 4–6

1 ⅓ cups whole kernel corn (fresh – see page 34 – or canned)	*1 ¼ cups béchamel sauce (see page 155), made with half milk and half light cream*
¾ pound broccoli	*bunch of fresh summer herbs of your choice, e.g. tarragon, thyme, dill, chopped*
¾ pound zucchini	
¾ pound carrots	
¼ pound thin green beans	*½ pound frozen or homemade puff pastry (see page 178)*
3 small leeks	

Steam all the vegetables separately until they are tender but still slightly crisp. Alternatively, cook them in the microwave. Let cool, reserving cooking juices, then chop into bite-size pieces.

Thin out the béchamel sauce with about ⅔ cup of the cooking juices. Stir in all the vegetables and herbs and pour into a large baking dish.

Roll out the pastry to a round or other shape that is 1 inch larger than the diameter of the dish. With the trimmings make a long thin strip of pastry. Moisten the rim of the dish and place this strip on it. Moisten the strip, then place the crust on top and press down with a fork to seal the edge.

Bake in a preheated 400°F oven until the pastry is risen and golden, 30–40 minutes.

CLASSIC TURNOVERS ❧

Nothing could be easier or cheaper than these tasty turnovers. Made in the classic way, they need a lot of tomato ketchup to go with them, and are a very satisfying supper dish.

MAKES 4

1 ⅔ cups vegetarian mince	*double recipe quantity easy piecrust dough (see page 179)*
1 cup each grated potato, turnip, and carrot	*milk*
sea salt and freshly ground black pepper	
4 tbsp water	

Mix the vegetarian mince with the grated vegetables and season with salt and pepper. Roll out the piecrust dough and cut into four 8-inch circles; or you can make 8 little turnovers, using 5-inch circles. Divide the mince mixture among the circles, placing it in a heap in the center. Add ½–1 tbsp water to each. Moisten the dough edges, then fold over into crescent shapes. Press the edges together, turn them, and crimp with a fork to make sure they are well sealed. Brush with milk and place on a well-greased baking sheet.

Bake in a preheated 425°F oven for 10 minutes, then turn the temperature down to 350°F and bake 15 minutes longer. Let cool a little on a rack, then lift carefully off the baking sheet to serve.

LIGHT SPINACH AND CHEESE PIE

This double-crust pie makes a delicious meal served with scalloped potatoes (see page 107) and zucchini with corn (page 43). Good, honest country food.

FOR 4

1 onion, chopped	*sea salt and freshly ground*
1 tbsp olive oil	*black pepper*
4 cups cooked spinach, well drained and chopped	*grated nutmeg*
⅔ cup béchamel sauce (see page 155)	*1 recipe quantity easy piecrust dough (see page 179)*
1 cup shredded cheese	*1 free-range egg yolk, beaten*

Soften the onion in the oil for 5–6 minutes, covered with a lid. Add the spinach and mix well, then stir in the béchamel. Mix in the shredded cheese. Season with salt, pepper, and nutmeg. Set aside.

Roll out about two-thirds of the piecrust dough and line a greased 8-inch pie pan, leaving a raised rim around the edge. Pour the spinach filling into the pastry shell. Roll out the rest of the dough into a round ½-inch larger in diameter than the top of the pan. Moisten the edge of the bottom crust, place the top crust carefully over the filling and crimp the edges together tightly. Press down with a fork to seal. Brush the top with beaten egg yolk.

Bake in a preheated 400°F oven until the pastry is golden, 30–35 minutes. Serve hot or warm.

BEST VEGETABLE QUICHE

A quiche is always a winner – a crisp pastry case holding a lovely creamy vegetable filling. The version here is made with zucchini. Alternative vegetables include: broccoli florets, sliced mushrooms, thinly sliced leeks, chopped artichoke bottoms, cauliflower florets, and spinach. Quiches freeze well so can be a useful standby.

FOR 6

1 recipe quantity easy piecrust dough (see page 179)	*2 tsp garam masala or to taste (optional)*
1¼ pounds small zucchini, thinly sliced	*3 free-range eggs*
4 tbsp margarine	*1 cup light cream*
2 large cloves garlic, finely sliced	*sea salt*

Roll out the piecrust dough and line a greased 8-inch loose-bottomed tart or quiche pan. Bake blind until part cooked (see page 115). Let cool.

Sauté the zucchini in the margarine until soft and turning golden brown. Remove from the heat and mix in the garlic and optional garam masala. Beat the eggs thoroughly with the cream and season with a little salt.

Arrange the zucchini in overlapping rings in the pastry shell, then carefully pour the cream and egg mixture over the top. Bake in a preheated 425°F oven for 30 minutes. Cool on a wire rack for at least 10 minutes before lifting the quiche carefully out of the pan.

CHEESE AND BROCCOLI QUICHE

This distinctive quiche, with the tangy flavor of goat cheese, makes a memorable lunch, or is excellent on a picnic. You can use ricotta or cheddar if you prefer a softer taste, and you can substitute cauliflower for broccoli as a variation.

FOR 6

1 recipe quantity easy piecrust dough (see page 179)	*¼ pound goat cheese, sliced*
1 large onion, chopped	*4 free-range eggs*
1 tbsp olive oil	*⅔ cup skim milk or light cream*
¾ pound broccoli florets	*3-4 tbsp skim or soy milk*
sea salt and freshly ground black pepper	

Roll out the piecrust dough and line a greased 9- or 10-inch loose-bottomed tart or quiche pan. Bake blind until part cooked.

Soften the onion in the oil, covered with a lid, for 5 minutes. Steam the broccoli florets until tender but still slightly crisp, 5–6 minutes. Mix them with the onion and season with salt and pepper. Spread over the bottom of the pastry shell and intersperse with the slices of cheese.

Beat the eggs thoroughly and stir in the milk or cream plus the extra milk. Season to taste with salt and pepper. Pour the mixture over the broccoli. Bake in a preheated 400°F oven until lightly browned and set, about 30 minutes. Serve hot or warm.

Baking Blind

Baking blind means baking a pastry shell before it is filled. If after the filling is put in, the tart, quiche, etc. is to be baked further, then the pastry shell is baked blind only until it is part cooked. If no further baking is to be done after the filling is added, the pastry shell is baked blind until it is completely cooked.

Roll out the piecrust dough on a lightly floured board and line the pan. Press the dough lightly into the corners and edges, and trim the edge. Prick the bottom with a fork in several places, then spread a piece of foil smoothly over the bottom and sides of the pastry shell; the foil should overlap the rim of the pan by 2 inches. Fill with baking beans. (You can buy ceramic baking beans, or simply use dried beans that you keep for this use alone – once baked they cannot be cooked.)

Bake in a preheated 400°F oven until just set, 10–15 minutes, then remove the beans and foil. Return to the oven (without the foil and beans) and bake five minutes longer to crisp and brown the pastry slightly. The pastry shell is now part cooked. To bake completely, return to the oven (without the foil and beans) and bake until the pastry is firm and brown, about 15 minutes.

OPPOSITE: Cheese and Broccoli Quiche

VEGETABLE MILLE-FEUILLES WITH PESTO

Mille-feuilles don't necessarily have to be the domain of sweet pâtisserie – savory ones are wonderful, too: elegant, appetizing food that melts in the mouth.

FOR 4

1 pound frozen or homemade puff pastry (see page 178)	*For the vegetable filling:*
1 free-range egg, beaten	*1½ pounds mixed vegetables, e.g. asparagus, snow peas, broccoli florets, green peas, zucchini, corn, spinach*
	1 cup crème fraîche
	2 tbsp pesto sauce (see page 149)

Roll the pastry out thinly and cut it into 8 rectangles, each measuring 2 x 5 inches. Brush each one with beaten egg and place on a well-greased baking sheet. Bake in a preheated 400°F oven until well risen and golden, 8–10 minutes. Split the pastry puffs horizontally about one-third of the way up their height, and keep hot.

Cut the vegetables into short lengths or small cubes and steam them until they are tender but still crisp. Mix together the crème fraîche and pesto and fold in the vegetables so that they are lightly coated. Heat through gently.

Pile the vegetable filling on the bottom layer of each mille-feuille and cover with the top layer of pastry. Serve immediately.

EASY LEEK PUFFS

You can vary the filling for these delectably light puff pastry triangles throughout the seasons – broccoli, zucchini, green peas, spinach, and mushrooms all make tasty fillings. They are wonderfully easy to make, and a firm favorite whenever they appear.

FOR 4

¾ pound leeks, chopped and cooked	*1 pound frozen or homemade puff pastry (see page 178)*
1¼ cups béchamel sauce (see page 155)	*1 free-range egg yolk, beaten*
¼ cup shredded cheddar cheese	

Stir the leeks into the béchamel, mixing thoroughly. Stir in the shredded cheese.

Roll out the puff pastry fairly thinly and cut it into four 5-inch squares. Moisten the edges with water. Place one-quarter of the leek mixture in the center of each square. Take one corner and fold it over to the opposite corner. Press the edges of the triangle together with a fork, so that they are well sealed. Brush the tops with beaten egg yolk and place on a well-greased baking sheet.

Bake in a preheated 425°F oven until risen and golden, 20–25 minutes.

EASY PIZZA

*A*homemade pizza is hard to beat, and makes a satisfying and delicious meal for all the family. Serve with a simple leafy salad tossed with the garlic mustard dressing on page 146.

FOR 4

For the dough:	For the topping:
1 package fast-rising dry yeast	*2 tbsp tomato paste*
2 cups all-purpose flour	*¾ pound ripe tomatoes, sliced*
⅛ tsp salt	*1 tbsp mixed dried thyme, oregano, and basil*
½–⅔ cup warm water	
1 tbsp olive oil	*sea salt and freshly ground black pepper*
	optional garnishes: sliced fresh hot chile pepper, red onion rings, black olives
	6 ounces mozzarella cheese, sliced, or goat cheese, grated

To make the dough, mix the yeast with the flour and salt and stir in enough warm water to make a soft dough. Knead thoroughly for 10–15 minutes. Halfway through this time, add the olive oil.

Press out the dough in a well-greased 11-inch metal pizza pan. Cover with a cloth and let rise in a warm place for 1 hour.

Spread the tomato paste over the dough and arrange the tomato slices on top. Sprinkle with the herbs and season with salt and pepper. If using chile or red onion rings, scatter them on top. Cover with the sliced cheese and add olives, if using.

Bake in a preheated 425°F oven until the base is well cooked and the topping browned, 20–25 minutes.

OTHER IDEAS FOR TOPPINGS:

- red onions, blue cheese, and rosemary
- grilled eggplant and simple pesto v
- leeks, tomatoes, and goat cheese
- roasted eggplant and mozzarella
- multicolor bell peppers, tomatoes, and mozzarella
- wild mushrooms, garlic, and herbs v
- artichoke hearts, onions, and cheese

117

CHAPTER SIX

Barbecues

Usually people associate barbecues with a lot of meat, but now that meat analogues are so good, and so widely available, even the most committed of carnivores will enjoy a meatless barbecue. You can grill vegetarian sausages, you can skewer vegetarian steak chunks onto mixed vegetable kebabs, and you can grill meatless patties and other products that come straight from your pantry or freezer to the hot coals. I usually coat veggie burgers, hot dogs, and so on with my tasty barbecue sauce. You can't beat it!

There are plenty of vegetables that barbecue very successfully – eggplant cooks beautifully over hot coals, as do zucchini, mushrooms, and potatoes. Corn on the cob is wonderful. You can marinate all of these in barbecue sauce, or just brush them with olive oil, and they are mouthwatering. Grilled halloumi cheese is irresistible, too.

Serve these with a tempting variety of salads (see pages 128 to 147 for ideas) and lots of tasty sauces, home-made salsas, and dips (pages 149 to 157).

MARINATED VEGETARIAN SAUSAGES AND BURGERS ♥

*M*y piquant, garlicky barbecue sauce is perfect for brushing onto vegetarian sausages and burgers before cooking. For extra flavor, make your fire with mesquite or other aromatic woods, or use a good charcoal.

FOR 6–8

vegetarian sausages and burgers	*buns to serve*
barbecue sauce (see page 153)	

Brush the sausages and burgers with barbecue sauce and, unless you are using frozen ones, let marinate if you have the time.

When the fire is ready, put your sausages and burgers on the grill and brown them, then flip them over and brown the other side. Vegetarian burgers and sausages don't need as long to cook as meat because they are not so tough!

Serve in buns with more barbecue sauce or with any other goodies from this section or others.

VEGETABLE KEBABS ♥

*C*olorful combinations of vegetables make beautiful kebabs, which you can vary endlessly using multicolored bell peppers, tomatoes, zucchini, etc. – whatever is in high season. The kebabs are delicious with barbecued veggie burgers and a potato salad (see page 130). Serve with a variety of sauces such as barbecue (page 153), chili (page 152), wild mushroom (page 154), or roasted red pepper (page 149).

FOR 6–8

½ pound medium carrots, cut in chunks	*3 small ears of corn, shucked and cut across in 1-inch slices*
1 small head cauliflower, separated into florets	*milk or soy milk*
6 ounces snow peas, trimmed	*vegetarian sausages, burgers, etc., cut in chunks (optional)*
6 ounces baby onions, peeled	*olive oil*

Cook all the vegetables separately in boiling water to which you have added 1 tbsp milk, until they are tender but still slightly crisp. Drain in a colander under cold running water.

Thread the pieces of vegetable onto skewers, alternating the colors. Include the chunks of vegetarian sausages, etc. if you are using them. Brush with oil, and grill on the rack over hot coals for 5 minutes, turning frequently.

CHAR-GRILLED MUSHROOMS WITH
ROSEMARY AND GARLIC ♥

ushrooms take on the woody flavor of charcoal exceptionally well, and are always popular as part of a barbecue meal. I've used fresh shiitake mushrooms here, but you could just as easily substitute large common mushrooms.

Trim the mushroom stems. Mix the remaining ingredients together and toss the mushrooms to coat. Let marinate up to 30 minutes.

Grill on the rack over hot coals about 3 minutes on each side, and serve hot.

FOR 3–4

½ pound fresh shiitake mushrooms	1 tsp minced fresh rosemary or ½ tsp dried rosemary
1 tbsp olive oil	freshly ground black pepper
1 tbsp soy sauce	
3 cloves garlic, minced	

GRILLED MARINATED VEGETABLES ♥

arbecued vegetables are scrumptious, particularly when they are marinated in this Japanese sauce which you can buy in bottles from most supermarkets. You can also just brush the vegetables with plenty of olive oil before grilling them.

Cut the vegetables into bite-size pieces and thread them onto skewers, alternating the colors. Mix the teriyaki sauce with the garlic and basil, add the skewers, and let marinate 20–30 minutes.

Put the skewers on the rack over hot coals and grill about 5 minutes, turning from time to time.

FOR 6

6 large flat mushrooms	⅔ cup teriyaki sauce
3 bell peppers	1 clove garlic, minced
6 zucchini, cut in half lengthwise	4-5 fresh basil leaves, chopped, or a large pinch chopped fresh tarragon
2 red onions, thickly sliced	

GRILLED NUT-TOPPED TOMATOES

These juicy tomatoes, covered with a layer of herbs, nuts, and cheese, make a delicious accompaniment to barbecued vegetarian sausages or burgers. The arugula and spinach salad on page 129 will complete the feast.

FOR 4 or 6

4 beefsteak or other large tomatoes	2 tbsp grated cheese, preferably Parmesan
sea salt and freshly ground black pepper	1 cup finely ground roasted peanuts, almonds, or other nuts of choice
soy sauce	margarine
1 tbsp chopped fresh basil or tarragon	
1 tbsp chopped parsley	

Cut the tomatoes in half crosswise and season the cut surfaces with salt and pepper. Sprinkle each half with a few drops of soy sauce. Mix the chopped basil or tarragon and parsley together and place on top, then sprinkle with the cheese. Cover with the ground nuts, patting on gently, and top each half with a small piece of margarine.

Wrap loosely in foil and place cut-side up on the barbecue rack over hot coals. Grill until the tomatoes are soft and hot, 20–25 minutes.

CHAR-GRILLED EGGPLANT ▾

Slices of eggplant marinated in herbs and oil take on the flavor of charcoal really well. They turn very soft and are wonderful with crisp barbecued vegetarian sausages and the avocado, mozzarella, and tomato salad on page 134.

FOR 6

2 large eggplants	sea salt and freshly ground black pepper
olive oil	
chopped fresh herbs	

Cut the eggplants diagonally into ½-inch slices. Mix the olive oil with herbs, salt, and pepper and brush over the cut sides of the eggplant slices. Let marinate up to 1 hour, basting and turning occasionally.

Grill on the rack over hot coals until the eggplant is soft and well cooked, about 5–6 minutes on each side.

Serve with sauces of your choice (see pages 149 to 153).

NEXT SPREAD: Vegetarian burgers and sausages with (clockwise from top left) Special Arugula Salad with Spinach and Parmesan, Balsamic Garlic and Herb Dressing, Chili Sauce, Barbecue Sauce, Char-grilled Eggplant and Zucchini with Herbs, Char-grilled Mushrooms, Vegetable Kebabs, and Potatoes with Sage and Cream

ZUCCHINI WITH HERBS ♥

Small zucchini marinated with herbs, garlic, and ginger give out wonderful aromas as they are basted on the barbecue. They go beautifully with barbecued vegetarian sausages, and the watercress salad with garlic croutons on page 136.

FOR 8

8 small zucchini, trimmed	2 dried bay leaves, crumbled
2 cloves garlic, minced	¼ cup fresh lemon juice
1 tbsp grated fresh ginger	3 tbsp olive oil
6 fresh mint leaves, chopped	salt
1 tsp chopped fresh marjoram	lemon slices and fresh herbs for garnish
1 tsp chopped fresh lemon verbena or lemon balm	

Run the tip of a sharp knife along the zucchini to score them.

Mix the garlic, ginger, and herbs with the lemon juice and oil and season with a little salt. Turn the zucchini in the mixture until thoroughly coated, then let marinate 4–5 hours, turning occasionally.

Remove the zucchini from the marinade and grill on the rack over hot coals until tender but still "al dente," 8–10 minutes. Turn and baste with the marinade frequently.

Serve skewered on wooden sticks, garnished with lemon slices and sprigs of fresh herbs.

POTATOES WITH SAGE AND CREAM

Potatoes baked in foil, nestled in the hot coals, have a quality all their own, and topping them with this sage-flavored sour cream sauce makes them even more delectable. Brilliant with char-grilled vegetarian sausages, plus a couple of salads such as the green bean salad on page 141 and carrot salad on page 134. Substitute chives for the sage as a variation.

FOR 6

6 baking potatoes, scrubbed	1 tbsp mild mustard
olive oil	sea salt and freshly ground black pepper
3 tbsp white wine vinegar	¾ cup sour cream
bunch of green onions, finely sliced	1 tbsp chopped fresh sage
1 free-range egg yolk	fresh sage leaves for garnish

Rub the potatoes with oil and wrap in double-thickness or heavy-duty foil. Bake in the hot coals until soft, 45 minutes to 1 hour, turning occasionally.

To make the sauce, put the vinegar in a small saucepan with the green onions and cook gently until the vinegar has almost evaporated. Remove the pan from the heat. Beat together the egg yolk, mustard, salt, and pepper, and stir into the green onions. The mixture will thicken immediately. Stir in the sour cream and minced sage and mix well. Keep hot.

Cut a deep cross in the top of each baked potato and squeeze the sides to open them out. Spoon in some sauce and serve garnished with sage leaves.

COUNTRY MUSHROOMS v

The rustic flavor of horseradish in the marinade permeates the mushrooms in this very simple recipe. Great as part of a large mixed barbecue menu along with vegetable kebabs (see page 119), sage and cream potatoes (page 124), and a selection of salads and sauces.

FOR 6 or 12

⅔ cup virgin olive oil	*12 flat mushrooms, stems removed*
4 tbsp horseradish sauce	
sea salt and freshly ground black pepper	*chopped parsley for garnish*

Mix together the olive oil and horseradish sauce in a soup plate or shallow dish and season to taste. Add the mushrooms and spoon the liquid over them until they are completely coated. Let marinate a minimum of 30 minutes, basting occasionally.

Grill on the rack over hot coals about 10 minutes, turning and basting occasionally. Garnish the open sides of the mushrooms with chopped parsley before serving.

CRUSTY GARLIC POTATOES

New potatoes stuffed with slivers of garlic and char-grilled with a crust of cornmeal make a very tasty dish to go with barbecued vegetarian burgers and a Caesar salad (see page 133). Delicious with the chili sauce on page 152.

FOR 4–6

1 pound new potatoes, scrubbed	*2 free-range eggs, beaten*
3-4 large cloves garlic, peeled	*about ½ cup yellow cornmeal*
	sprigs of parsley for garnish

Cook the potatoes in boiling salted water until tender, 12–15 minutes. Drain and let cool slightly. Slice the garlic thickly and, using the tip of a sharp knife or skewer, insert deeply into the potatoes. Dip the potatoes first in beaten egg and then in cornmeal to coat all over.

Grill on the rack over hot coals until crusty and golden, 10–15 minutes, turning occasionally and taking care that the cornmeal doesn't burn. Serve in a basket lined with a clean napkin, garnished with sprigs of parsley.

PEACHES AND BUTTERSCOTCH

*T*hese make an irresistible finale to a barbecue party – peaches filled with ground almonds, baked over the coals, and served with a creamy butterscotch sauce.

FOR 6 or 12

	For the butterscotch sauce:
6 peaches, cut in half and pit removed	*½ cup firmly packed light brown sugar*
⅔ cup ground almonds	*⅔ cup maple syrup*
	3 tbsp margarine
	pinch of salt
	⅔ cup light cream
	1 tsp vanilla extract

To make the sauce, combine the sugar, maple syrup, margarine, and salt in a heavy-bottomed saucepan. Bring to a boil, stirring to dissolve the sugar, and boil until the mixture is thick, about 3 minutes. Stir in the cream and bring back to a boil, then remove from the heat immediately and stir in the vanilla. Set aside.

Put the peach halves, cut-side down, on squares of double-thickness or heavy-duty foil. Curl the edges of the foil up around the fruit and place on the rack over hot coals. Cook 5 minutes.

Turn the peach halves over on the foil and spoon the ground almonds into the hollows. Pour 1 heaping tbsp of the butterscotch sauce over each half. Carefully draw up the edges of the foil over the top, and seal. Cook over the coals until tender, about 10 minutes longer. Serve hot with the remaining butterscotch sauce.

PRALINE BANANAS ♥

*B*arbecuing bananas in their skins is a revelation. You can cook them over the coals very simply, with no extras, and serve them with whipped cream or ice cream. Or you can split the skins, insert slices of chocolate, and heat over the coals until it melts. Here, crunchy praline is added, to devastating effect.

FOR 6

2 tbsp shelled almonds	*6 under-ripe bananas*
2 tbsp shelled hazelnuts	*whipped cream or thick yogurt to serve*
¼ cup sugar	

Put the nuts and sugar in a small heavy-bottomed skillet and heat gently, stirring until the sugar dissolves. Turn the heat up and cook to a deep brown syrup. Immediately pour onto a sheet of parchment paper placed on a metal baking sheet on a wooden board. Leave until cold and brittle, then crush finely.

Lay the unpeeled bananas flat and make a slit in the skin along the top. Slightly open out the skin and add about 1 tbsp praline to each banana. Wrap up tightly in double-thickness or heavy-duty foil and seal along the top. Cook directly on medium-hot coals for 8–10 minutes, turning halfway through the cooking time. Serve in the skins, with whipped cream or thick yogurt.

OPPOSITE: Peaches and Butterscotch

CHAPTER SEVEN

Salads

*E*ating fresh, raw ingredients has been shown to be very beneficial to health, and is recommended as part of the daily diet. You can eat salads as main dishes, as first courses, or as a side dish to go with a cooked dish. Full of vitamins and minerals, which are sometimes reduced or destroyed with cooking, salads give us a feeling of vitality and energy that many other foods do not.

A salad can be an art-form. The colors, textures, and shapes of the kaleidoscope of ingredients combine to make endless pleasures for the table. Bell peppers come in yellow, red, orange, green, cream, and even purple. The cream or very pale green of cauliflower next to the dark green spinach leaf; the russet of red-leaved lettuce alongside fresh greenery; baby carrots, sun-dried tomatoes, raw mushrooms, beans and lentils of all colors, deep red beets – all these make up the palette for the artistic cook.

SUN-DRIED TOMATO AND CHICK PEA SALAD ♥

A garlicky dressing and the sweet-sharpness of cooked red onion in vinegar give this unusual salad memorable qualities. Serve with warm pita bread as a light lunch dish or a first course.

FOR 4–6

½ small red onion, finely chopped

1 tbsp white wine vinegar

¼ cup red wine vinegar

1 clove garlic, minced

sea salt and freshly ground black pepper

2 tbsp extra virgin olive oil

1 can (16 ounces) chick peas (garbanzo beans), drained (or equivalent cooked dried, see page 185)

⅓ cup diced sun-dried tomatoes packed in oil

2-3 tbsp chopped fresh parsley or tarragon

2 tbsp fresh lemon juice

Bring a small saucepan of water to a boil, add the onion, and cook 30 seconds. Drain, and toss with the white wine vinegar.

Mix together with the red wine vinegar, garlic, salt, and pepper and gradually whisk in the oil. Toss the chick peas, sun-dried tomatoes, and onion with the dressing and let marinate 1 hour.

Add the chopped parsley or tarragon and lemon juice, toss to mix, and serve at room temperature.

SPECIAL ARUGULA SALAD WITH SPINACH AND PARMESAN

A salad of assertive flavors, this mixture of arugula and spinach in a simple dressing of olive oil and lemon juice makes a wonderful side dish or first course. Cheese shavings scattered over the top give added distinction.

FOR 2–3

5 ounces arugula leaves

6 ounces young spinach leaves

sea salt

¼ cup extra virgin olive oil

2 tbsp fresh lemon juice, or to taste

1½ ounces Parmesan or any favorite cheese, pared finely into shavings or grated

Prepare the arugula and spinach leaves, put them in a salad bowl, and sprinkle with sea salt. Mix the olive oil with the lemon juice, add to the leaves, and toss to coat. Scatter the shavings of Parmesan on top and it is ready to serve.

POTATO AND ROMAINE WITH GARLIC VINAIGRETTE ˅

The slightly bitter flavor of romaine lettuce goes beautifully with the bland delicacy of potato, in a delicious garlicky dressing. Chopped chives are a perfect finishing touch.

FOR 4-6

2 large cloves garlic, minced	*1 head romaine lettuce, coarsely shredded*
⅓ cup vinaigrette (see page 146)	*1 small red onion, finely chopped*
2 pounds new potatoes, scrubbed	*chopped fresh chives for garnish*

Stir the garlic into the vinaigrette and let stand while you prepare the rest.

Cook the potatoes in boiling salted water until just tender but still firm in the center. Drain, and rinse under cold water. Let cool, then cut in small cubes or slices.

Combine the potatoes, shredded romaine, and minced onion in a salad bowl. Toss with the vinaigrette until well mixed and let stand 20–30 minutes. Scatter chopped chives over the top just before serving.

POTATO SALAD

A delectable salad for all seasons: firm potatoes, crunchy celery, plus some green onions in a lemony mayonnaise scented with fresh dill and parsley.

FOR 4

1½ pounds small new potatoes, scraped or scrubbed	*large handful of fresh dill, chopped*
4 stalks celery, chopped	*small bunch of parsley, chopped*
6 green onions, finely sliced	*1 dill pickle, chopped (optional)*
2-3 tbsp fresh lemon juice	
⅓-½ cup bottled or homemade mayonnaise (see page 150)	

Cook the potatoes in boiling salted water until just tender but still firm in the center. Let cool, and cut in cubes. Mix with the celery and green onions.

Add lemon juice to the mayonnaise, flavoring it so that it is quite sharp. Stir in the chopped dill and mix thoroughly. Toss the potatoes in the dressing until well coated. Put into a salad bowl and garnish with chopped parsley and dill pickle (if using).

OPPOSITE: Potato and Romaine with Garlic Vinaigrette

WARM GOAT CHEESE SALAD

This salad makes a lovely first course for a summer meal, especially served with hot garlic bread. Many goat cheeses are made without the use of animal rennet, and will say so on the packaging.

FOR 4

1 head crisp lettuce	*4 sun-dried tomatoes packed in oil, finely sliced*
2 handfuls of fresh young spinach leaves	*2 tbsp chopped mild onion*
bunch of watercress	*6 ounces creamy goat cheese*
handful of small radicchio leaves	*olive oil*
3 tbsp vinaigrette (see page 146)	

Prepare all the salad leaves and toss them in the vinaigrette with the sun-dried tomatoes and onion. Divide among four plates. Slice the goat cheese into rounds and brush them with olive oil. Broil until they blister and turn slightly golden, then place on top of the salads and serve immediately, with warm French bread.

Keeping Salad Fresh

Cut or torn salad leaves, washed and dried in a salad spinner, will keep crisp longer if they are stored in an airtight bag in the refrigerator.

CAESAR SALAD

Deservedly a classic, Caesar salad can be served as a first course or side dish, particularly with barbecues in high summer. It can be a light meal in itself, too, with just some warm whole-wheat bread.

FOR 4

3 slices bread, crusts removed	*For the dressing:*
oil for frying	*2 tbsp balsamic vinegar*
1 large head crisp lettuce, preferably romaine	*1 tbsp lemon juice*
3 ounces lamb's lettuce (mâche)	*1 tbsp Dijon mustard*
8 green onions, trimmed	*¼ cup extra virgin olive oil*
¼ cup finely grated cheese	*1 large clove garlic, minced (optional)*

Cut the bread into small cubes and fry in hot oil until crisp and golden all over. Drain and cool on paper towels. Mix together the ingredients for the dressing.

Divide the lettuce into leaves and tear larger leaves into manageable pieces. Put into a bowl with the lamb's lettuce and green onions and sprinkle the cheese over the top. Toss with the dressing and fold the croutons in just before serving.

OPPOSITE: Warm Goat Cheese Salad

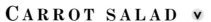

CARROT SALAD ♥

This salad is utterly simple, yet delicious, nutritious, and fresh. If you prefer a slightly stronger bite, you can use a red onion instead of the green onions.

FOR 4

8 medium carrots, grated	7 green onions, minced
⅓ cup chopped parsley	3 tbsp vinaigrette (see page 146)

Mix together the carrots, parsley, and green onions in a salad bowl. Dress with the vinaigrette and mix thoroughly.

FENNEL SALAD

This healthy, crunchy salad of fennel, carrot, apple, and radish is dressed in a lemony mayonnaise, which adds to its freshness. Food for vitality.

FOR 4–6

12 radishes, trimmed	1 tbsp fresh lemon juice
3 bulbs fennel, trimmed	½ cup bottled or homemade mayonnaise (see page 150)
2 medium carrots, peeled	
1 green-skinned apple, cored	

Make four vertical cuts, crossing in the center, in each radish. Soak in ice water until the "petals" open, 2–3 hours. Drain.

Cut the fennel bulbs lengthwise in half and cut out the hard core. Slice very finely. Cut the carrots into matchsticks. Dice the apple. Mix the lemon juice into the vegetables, and then toss with the mayonnaise. Pile into a salad bowl and garnish with the radishes.

AVOCADO, MOZZARELLA AND TOMATO SALAD

An Italian classic, this is a salad of complementary textures and contrasting rich colors.

FOR 4

2 ripe avocados, peeled and pit removed	1 pound ripe tomatoes
lemon juice	⅓ cup vinaigrette (see page 146)
½ pound mozzarella cheese	handful of fresh basil leaves

Slice the avocados and sprinkle immediately with lemon juice to prevent them from going brown. Slice the mozzarella and tomatoes.

Arrange the slices of green avocado, white cheese and red tomato decoratively in a shallow dish. Dribble the vinaigrette over the top and scatter the basil leaves over the salad just before serving.

OPPOSITE: Carrot Salad (left) and Fennel Salad

WATERCRESS SALAD WITH GARLIC CROUTONS ♥

An elegant combination of watercress and crisp lettuce dressed with vinaigrette, this delectable salad has the added treat of crunchy, garlicky croutons.

FOR 4

2 thick slices bread, crusts removed	*2 bunches of watercress*
1 clove garlic, cut in half	*handful of crisp lettuce leaves*
vegetable or olive oil for frying	*6 tbsp vinaigrette (see page 146)*

Cut the bread into small cubes. Rub the cut side of the garlic over the surface of a skillet, then discard the garlic. Heat enough oil for shallow frying in the skillet, about ½ inch, and fry the bread gently until golden brown all over. Remove with a slotted spoon and drain on paper towels.

Prepare the watercress and lettuce. Line a salad bowl with the lettuce leaves. Toss the watercress in the vinaigrette until well coated. Pile the watercress inside the lettuce leaves and scatter the croutons over the top.

SPICY RAW MUSHROOM SALAD

Sliced button mushrooms dressed in a lightly curried mayonnaise and sprinkled with fresh cilantro make an excellent first course, as well as a tasty addition to a buffet table.

FOR 3–4

¾ pound small button mushrooms	*1 tbsp fresh lemon juice*
2-3 tsp curry paste	*1 large clove garlic, minced (optional)*
⅓-½ cup bottled or homemade mayonnaise (see page 150)	*fresh cilantro leaves for garnish*

Slice the mushrooms. Mix the curry paste into the mayonnaise with the lemon juice and add the garlic, if desired. Fold in the mushrooms and mix thoroughly until they are well coated in the mayonnaise. Put into a serving dish and garnish with fresh cilantro leaves.

Peeling Garlic

Press down on the clove with the flat side of a knife blade, then pull away the burst skin.

OPPOSITE: Watercress Salad with Garlic Croutons

PROVENÇAL PEPPER SALAD ❧

This is a salad redolent of the Mediterranean, with its aromatic fresh herbs and the strong flavors of olives and peppers. Brightly colored, it makes a lovely luncheon dish. Vegans can use potato in place of the eggs.

FOR 6

1 tbsp each minced fresh parsley, tarragon, chervil, and chives	*2 red bell peppers*
	6 ripe tomatoes, sliced
1 recipe quantity vinaigrette (see page 146)	*4 hard-boiled eggs, shelled and sliced, or 1 cubed potato, cooked until just tender*
2 green bell peppers	*24 black olives*

Stir the herbs into the vinaigrette and let stand while you prepare the salad.

Peel the peppers (see page 59) and cut in long strips. Place the tomatoes in the bottom of a large, flat serving dish and drizzle one-quarter of the dressing over them. Arrange the pepper strips in a criss-cross pattern on the tomatoes and drizzle with half of the remaining dressing. Cover with the slices of hard-boiled egg and drizzle the rest of the vinaigrette over them. Decorate with olives before serving.

ROASTED PEPPERS WITH MUSHROOMS AND ARUGULA ❧

Juicy bell peppers, tender mushrooms, and the earthy flavor of arugula combine to make an original salad. The taste of balsamic vinegar in the garlicky dressing adds a special touch.

FOR 4–6

¾ pound small button mushrooms	*1 recipe quantity balsamic garlic dressing (see page 146)*
1 red or yellow bell pepper, peeled (see page 59) and cut in thick strips	*2 large handfuls of arugula*
	8-12 green olives, pitted
2 tbsp capers, drained	

Cut the mushrooms in half, unless they are very tiny. Mix together with the pepper strips and capers, and toss with all but 2 tbsp of the dressing. Let marinate 20–30 minutes.

Prepare the arugula and toss with the remaining dressing. Place in the bottom of a salad bowl and arrange the vegetables on top. Garnish with the olives and serve.

OPPOSITE: Provençal Pepper Salad

CAULIFLOWER SALAD WITH MUSTARD MAYONNAISE

A simple salad with a definite flavor, this is excellent fare at any time of year, useful for a party or buffet table. It would go well with zucchini with corn (see page 43) to make a light meal.

FOR 4

2 medium potatoes, peeled and cubed	*2 tbsp fresh lemon juice*
1 small head cauliflower, cut into florets	*2 tbsp plain set yogurt*
	1 tbsp chopped fresh tarragon
1 tbsp whole-grain mustard	*2 stalks celery, sliced*
¼ cup bottled or homemade mayonnaise (see page 150)	*chopped parsley for garnish*

Steam the potatoes until just tender. Steam the cauliflower florets until they are slightly cooked but still crunchy, 4–5 minutes. Let cool, and slice them.

Mix the mustard into the mayonnaise, add the lemon juice, and stir in the yogurt and the tarragon. Toss the potato, cauliflower, and celery gently with this dressing and put into a dish. Sprinkle with the chopped parsley.

BEET SALAD WITH SOUR CREAM AND GARLIC

A wonderful salad for winter, with rich flavors and beautiful colors – red, pink, and green. Cooked beets are an excellent addition to many salads; here they play the starring role.

FOR 4

1 ½ pounds beets, cooked and peeled	*3 cloves garlic, minced*
	freshly ground black pepper
⅔ cup sour cream	*1 tbsp chopped fresh parsley or tarragon*
1 tbsp lemon juice	

Cut the prepared beets into medium-thin slices. Mix the sour cream with the lemon juice and garlic and season with pepper. Dress the beets, mixing gently until well coated. Pile into a salad bowl and sprinkle with the chopped parsley.

GREEN BEAN SALAD ♥

A salad for summer when green beans come into season, this combination with red onion, dill, and garlic is a treat. Capers add an unusual touch.

Steam the prepared beans lightly, so that they are still very crisp. Mix with the dill, onion, garlic, and capers, and season lightly with salt and pepper. Dress with the vinaigrette, mix well, and serve.

FOR 4-6

1 pound string beans or other green beans, trimmed	*1 small clove garlic, minced*
	1/3 cup capers, drained
3 tbsp chopped fresh dill or 1 1/2 tbsp dried dill	*sea salt and freshly ground black pepper*
1 small red onion, finely diced	*1/3 cup vinaigrette (see page 146)*

SHREDDED ZUCCHINI SALAD ♥

A fresh and simple salad for late summer when zucchini are at their best. Fresh ginger, capers, and pine nuts add an unusual piquant note. Serve with warm garlic bread.

Grate the zucchini and pat dry with paper towels. Combine the lemon juice, olive oil, garlic, ginger, salt, and pepper in a small jar and shake to blend. Pour the dressing over the zucchini and add the capers and pine nuts. Mix thoroughly and serve immediately. (If left to stand it will go watery.)

FOR 6

4 medium zucchini, trimmed	*1 tbsp grated fresh ginger*
3 tbsp fresh lemon juice	*sea salt and freshly ground black pepper*
2 tbsp extra virgin olive oil	
1 medium clove garlic, minced	*2 tbsp capers, drained*
	2-3 tbsp pine nuts

TECHNICOLOR BEAN SALAD ᵥ

A bright salad with interesting flavors, this is tossed in a very garlicky vinaigrette. It makes an excellent addition to a buffet table, or it can be served as a first course.

FOR 6

2 cans (16 ounces each) mixed beans (or equivalent cooked dried beans such as navy or cannellini, black-eyed peas, red kidney beans, etc., see page 185)	For the garlic dressing:
	juice of ½ lemon
	2-3 tbsp wine vinegar
	1 tsp sea salt
	4 large cloves garlic, minced
½ pound green beans, trimmed	*freshly ground black pepper*
	⅔ cup extra virgin olive oil
6-8 green onions, chopped	
medium bunch of parsley, finely chopped	

To make the dressing, mix together the lemon juice, vinegar, salt, and garlic in a bowl and add lots of freshly ground black pepper. Stirring all the time, dribble in the olive oil so that the dressing thickens as you mix it. Check the seasoning.

Drain the canned beans and rinse them. Drain thoroughly. Steam the green beans until just tender, 5–6 minutes. Toss all the beans together with the green onions, then add the garlic dressing and toss again. Sprinkle the chopped parsley over the top. Serve at room temperature.

PASTA AND BEAN SALAD WITH BASIL AND PECORINO

A n alluring mixture of bell peppers, green beans and kidney beans, pasta, and herbs, this salad's finishing touch is finely pared cheese. It's really a meal in itself, served with warm fresh bread.

FOR 6

½ pound bow-tie pasta	*¼ cup chopped parsley*
1 red bell pepper, peeled (see page 59) and cut in thin slices	*1 recipe quantity soy and lemon dressing (see page 147)*
1 yellow bell pepper, peeled (see page 59) and cut in thin slices	*handful of fresh basil leaves, shredded*
6 ounces green beans, cooked	*2 ounces pecorino romano cheese, pared finely into shavings*
⅔ cup red kidney beans (canned or equivalent cooked dried, see page 185)	

Cook the bow-tie pasta in boiling water until "al dente" (see page 90). Drain, and rinse immediately under cold water in a colander.

Mix the bell peppers, pasta, green beans, kidney beans, and parsley in a salad bowl, add the dressing, and toss until thoroughly mixed together. Finally, fold in the basil and garnish with the pecorino shavings.

OPPOSITE: Technicolor Bean Salad with its dressing

CURRIED PASTA SALAD ♥

A main-dish salad with plenty of bite and zest. You can add chopped mango for an exotic touch, plus a garnish of fresh cilantro leaves if you like.

FOR 4

¾ pound pasta shells	For the dressing:
1 tsp olive oil	⅔ cup extra virgin olive oil
½ pound baby mushrooms	¼ cup white wine vinegar
3 green onions, chopped	2 tbsp fresh lemon juice
2 stalks celery, thinly sliced	2 tbsp light brown sugar
	1 ½ tbsp curry powder

Cook the pasta until "al dente" (see page 90), then drain thoroughly and rinse under cold water. Toss thoroughly with the oil, mixing with your hands so that the pasta shells are separated. Add the mushrooms, green onions, and celery.

Mix together the dressing ingredients, add to the pasta salad, and toss well. Refrigerate 1 hour or overnight, but serve at room temperature.

ORANGE RICE SALAD ♥

The unusual method of cooking rice in orange juice gives it an exceptional flavor. A tasty mixture of pimientos and snow peas, plus some red onion, is added to the rice to make up an unusual and delectable salad.

FOR 6

1 cup long-grain rice	¼ pound snow peas, trimmed and sliced
2 cups fresh orange juice	
2 canned pimientos, drained and cut in strips	2 large oranges, peeled and divided in sections
1 small red onion, minced	½ cup vinaigrette (see page 146)

Rinse the rice and put into a saucepan with the orange juice. Bring to a boil. Stir once, then cover tightly and cook very gently until the liquid is absorbed and the rice tender, about 15 minutes. Fluff it up with a fork and let cool in a bowl.

Mix the prepared vegetables into the cooled rice. Cut up the orange sections and mix them in. Toss thoroughly with the vinaigrette, and it is ready to serve.

SALAD DRESSINGS

Salad dressings can be made with a wide variety of oils and vinegars, plus flavorings such as garlic, fresh herbs, fresh ginger, and mustard. In some cases, you don't need to make the dressing beforehand, mixing it in a bowl or jar – just combine the ingredients in the bottom of the salad bowl, then add the salad and toss together.

Oils for salad dressings include:
• corn oil, which is odorless and very bland. It is high in polyunsaturates.
• peanut oil, which is clear and mild in flavor; the Chinese version has a distinctive taste of peanuts. Peanut oil is about 50 percent monounsaturated fat and 30 percent polyunsaturated.
• olive oil, which has a distinctive fruity flavor. Unrefined extra virgin oil is obtained from a first cold pressing of the olives; it has a stronger flavor and greener color than other olive oils, and is preferred for dressings. It is high in mono-unsaturated fat.
• sesame oil, expressed from sesame seeds, which gives an Asian flavoring. Light-colored sesame oil has a delicious nutty flavor; the darker oils are too strong for salad dressings. Sesame oil is high in polyunsaturates.
• sunflower oil, which has a delicate flavor and pale yellow color. It is very high in polyunsaturates.
• walnut oil, which has a nutty taste and fragrance.
   Other nuts pressed for oil include hazelnut and almond. Use these rich, strongly flavored oils sparingly, mixing them with a blander oil.

Vinegars to choose from include:
• cider, which has a clean, sharp, fruity taste. It is said to have health-giving properties.
• balsamic, a very fine vinegar from Italy, which is made from fermented grapes and aged in wood barrels. It is dark brown, thick, aromatic, and full-flavored, so is normally used in moderation.
• raspberry and other fruit vinegars, which are increasingly popular. They give a full fruity flavor and rich color.
• red wine, which is similar in flavor to white wine vinegar, but slightly mellower. It gives a denser, darker quality to a salad dressing.
• sherry, which has a distinctive flavor and aroma. It gives an unusual quality to dressings.
• white wine, one of the most commonly used. It gives a pungent tang to dressings. White wine vinegar is often infused with herbs, such as tarragon, rosemary, sage, and mint, as well as garlic or mixed herbs with chili.

The best herbs to use for salad dressings are basil, chives, cilantro, dill, fennel, marjoram, parsley, and thyme. For the maximum flavor, infuse the freshly chopped herb in the dressing for up to half an hour before using.

VINAIGRETTE ♥

*H*ere's a recipe for the basic dressing than can be used for almost any salad. Experiment with different oils, vinegars and mustards, to find the combination you like best, and vary the ingredients to suit the salads too.

FOR 4-6

1-2 tsp mild or whole-grain mustard	*sea salt and freshly ground black pepper*
2 tbsp fresh lemon juice	*5 tbsp extra virgin olive oil*
2 tbsp wine, balsamic, or cider vinegar	*minced garlic to taste (optional)*

Mix the mustard with the lemon juice and vinegar and season with salt and pepper. Stir in the olive oil gradually so that the dressing thickens as you mix. It should become creamy in consistency. Stir in the garlic (if using). Let stand up to 30 minutes before using, to allow the flavors to develop.

BALSAMIC GARLIC AND HERB DRESSING ♥

MAKES ½ CUP

3-4 tbsp balsamic vinegar	*1 tbsp chopped parsley*
2 cloves garlic, minced	*1 tsp chopped fresh tarragon or basil or any combination of your favorite herbs*
sea salt and freshly ground black pepper	
5 tbsp extra virgin olive oil	

Mix the balsamic vinegar with the garlic and seasoning to taste. Gradually add the olive oil, whisking all the time so that the dressing amalgamates. Mix in the herbs.

GARLIC MUSTARD DRESSING ♥

MAKES 1 ¾ CUPS

juice of ½ lemon	*6 cloves garlic, minced*
3-4 tbsp mild mustard	*1¼ cups extra virgin olive oil*
¼ cup red wine vinegar	
sea salt and freshly ground black pepper	

Put the lemon juice, mustard, and vinegar into the blender and season with salt and pepper. Blend until well mixed, then add the garlic. Start adding the olive oil in a dribble, gradually increasing to a slow, steady stream. When all the oil has been incorporated, check the seasoning. Store in an airtight container in the refrigerator.

You can also make this without a blender: stir vigorously with a whisk as you slowly add the oil in a thin stream.

POPPY SEED DRESSING ♥

MAKES 2 ½ CUPS

⅓ cup sugar or honey	*¼ cup grated sweet onion*
1 tbsp mild mustard	*1¾ cups extra virgin olive oil*
¼ cup red wine vinegar	*3-4 tbsp poppy seeds*
sea salt	*2 tbsp fresh lemon juice*

Combine the sugar or honey, mustard, vinegar, salt to taste, and grated onion in a food processor and run the machine for 1 minute. Then pour in the oil in a slow, steady stream with the machine running. When all the oil has been incorporated, check the seasoning. Stir in the poppy seeds and lemon juice. Keep refrigerated until ready to use.

SOY AND LEMON DRESSING ∨

MAKES ²/₃ CUP

juice of 1 lemon	*freshly ground black pepper*
3-4 tbsp soy sauce	*1 tsp grated fresh ginger*
6 tbsp dark sesame oil	*1 garlic clove, minced*

Mix all the ingredients together in a small bowl.

THOUSAND ISLAND DRESSING

MAKES 1¼ CUPS

1¼ cups bottled or homemade mayonnaise (see page 150)	*2-3 tbsp minced dill pickle or sweet pickle relish (optional)*
¼ cup tomato ketchup	*2 tbsp fresh lemon juice*
2 tbsp minced parsley (optional)	

Mix all the ingredients together and keep refrigerated until ready to use.

LEMONY CAPER VINAIGRETTE ∨

MAKES 1¼ CUPS

²/₃ cup extra virgin olive oil	*snipped fresh chives (optional)*
½ cup fresh lemon juice	*finely chopped shallots (optional)*
1 tbsp capers, drained and chopped	*sea salt and freshly ground black pepper*
1-2 tbsp mild mustard (optional)	

Combine all the ingredients in a screw-top jar and shake until well blended.

YOGURT DRESSING

FOR 4-6

½ cup plain yogurt	*minced green or red bell pepper (optional)*
2 tbsp fresh lemon juice	*sea salt and freshly ground black pepper*
1-2 tbsp grated mild onion	
1 tbsp celery seed	
minced garlic to taste	

Mix all the ingredients together and season to taste.

BLUE CHEESE DRESSING

MAKES ABOUT 1 CUP

1-2 tsp mild or whole-grain mustard	*2 ounces Danish blue cheese or another blue cheese, crumbled*
3 tbsp fresh lemon juice	*½ cup extra virgin olive oil*
2 tbsp wine vinegar	*freshly ground black pepper*

Mix the mustard with the lemon juice and vinegar. Add the crumbled cheese and mash thoroughly. Gradually add the olive oil, stirring until the dressing is completely smooth. Season to taste with lots of pepper.

Flower Garnishes

Many common flowers, both garden and wild, are edible. They make great additions to salads or to use as stunning garnishes. When your herbs flower in spring and early summer, add the flowers to your salads along with the chopped leaves. Lovely scented rose petals can be used as the summer progresses.

You can also choose from the following:
allium, apple blossoms, carnations and pinks, cornflowers, daisies, geraniums, gladioli, hawthorn, honeysuckle, hop flowers, hibiscus, jasmine, lavender, lilac, lime flowers, mallow, marigolds, nasturtiums, pansies, pea flowers, plum blossoms, radish flower, rosemary, snapdragons, summer squash, stocks, strawberry flowers, and violets.

CHAPTER EIGHT

Sauces and Dips

In many of the great cuisines of the world there are traditional sauces made purely with vegetables and dairy products. Hollandaise and mayonnaise are two well-known examples from classic French cooking; pesto from Italy and salsa from Mexico are two more that have caught the global imagination in recent years. Sweet and sour sauce from the East has long been widely loved, as has American barbecue sauce.

A good sauce will enhance the delicate flavors of meatless dishes, and adds elegance and interest to home-cooked meals. The recipes in this section are just a small sample of the enormous worldwide repertoire of sauces – sauces for pasta, sauces to go with meatless meatballs or loaf, sauces for pastry dishes, sauces for potatoes and other plainly cooked vegetables, and thicker sauces to be served as dips for raw vegetables, fruit, bread, and tortilla chips.

ROASTED RED PEPPER SAUCE

This sauce needs no seasoning – it has an absolutely amazing flavor, which comes from roasting the peppers, and the most beautiful color.

MAKES 1 1/4 CUPS

2 large red bell peppers	2 tbsp flour
1 1/4 cups vegetable stock	2-3 tbsp crème fraîche or light cream
2 tbsp margarine	

Cut the peppers in half and remove the seeds. Place on a baking pan and roast in a preheated 400°F oven for 15–20 minutes, then cool. Peel them, chop roughly, and blend with the stock to a thin purée.

Heat the margarine, stir in the flour, and gradually stir in the purée with a wooden spoon. When it is thickened and smooth, simmer gently for 3–4 minutes, then remove from the heat and stir in the crème fraîche or light cream.

TARRAGON AND MUSTARD SAUCE

A fine sauce that turns the simplest of meals into something special. Try it with the layered vegetable terrine on page 81, stuffed bell peppers (page 68), or the cottage crunch casserole on page 67.

MAKES 1 1/4 CUPS

2 tbsp margarine	1 tbsp cornstarch
1/3 cup chopped fresh tarragon or 2 tbsp dried tarragon	1/2 cup milk
1 tbsp mild mustard	2/3 cup crème fraîche or light cream

Melt the margarine and cook the tarragon in it very gently for 2–3 minutes. Stir in the mustard and mix well. Sprinkle in the cornstarch and stir until smooth, then gradually add the milk, stirring all the time. When the sauce is smooth and thick, stir in the crème fraîche.

SIMPLE PESTO SAUCE v

This version of pesto has no cheese or nuts in it, and it is simple, fresh, and irresistible. Serve with fresh pasta for a quick, delicious meal.

MAKES 1/4 CUP

8-10 large cloves garlic, minced or pressed	4 tbsp olive oil
2 large bunches of fresh basil, chopped	

Combine the ingredients in a bowl and stir together. Cover and chill before serving.

For traditional pesto, add 1/4 cup pine nuts and 3/4 cup freshly grated Parmesan cheese. Pound all the ingredients together with a mortar and pestle, or blend until creamy in a blender or food processor. Store in an airtight jar in the refrigerator.

HOLLANDAISE

An elegant sauce for steamed vegetables through the seasons, either hot or cold. It is also delicious with crudités as an appetizer. If you like, stir in a little crème fraîche or plain yogurt.

FOR 4

3 tbsp white wine vinegar	*fresh lemon juice to taste*
2 tbsp cold water	*sea salt and freshly ground*
3 free-range egg yolks, beaten	*black pepper*
¾ cup (6 ounces) margarine, warmed	

Boil the vinegar and water hard until reduced to 1 tbsp. Put into a bowl and place it over gently heating water in a saucepan. Add the egg yolks and stir thoroughly, then gradually stir in little portions of the margarine. Stir constantly. If the sauce thickens too quickly, add a few drops of cold water. Do not overheat. Season to taste with lemon juice, salt, and pepper.

MAYONNAISE

The homemade version of this most popular of sauces is superior to any bought one. Resist any temptation to add the oil faster than the recipe describes: it will not emulsify (thicken) well if you do.

MAKES 1¼ CUPS

1 free-range egg	*sea salt and freshly ground*
1 tsp Dijon mustard	*black pepper*
1¼ cups olive or sunflower oil	*fresh lemon juice to taste*

Break the egg into the bowl of the blender and add the mustard. Blend until well mixed, then start to add the oil drop by drop, with the machine running. After a while increase to a thin stream; as the mayonnaise thickens you can increase the flow of oil even more. When all the oil has been added, continue to blend for another minute to thicken the mayonnaise. Season to taste with salt, pepper, and lemon juice.

GREEN HERB MAYONNAISE

MAKES 1¼ CUPS

2 heaping tbsp chopped fresh tarragon or dill	*2 heaping tbsp chopped baby spinach leaves*
2 heaping tbsp each chopped parsley, chives, and watercress	*1¼ cups bottled or homemade mayonnaise (see left)*

Mince the herbs and leaves in the food processor. Add to the mayonnaise and stir in thoroughly.

The Food Processor

If you have not already got one, a food processor is perhaps the best investment you can make as a keen cook. It does so many things, and much faster than you can do them yourself. It makes wonderful smooth soups; it shreds vegetables in an instant; it makes vegetable purées without effort; it grates, slices and minces very very finely; it makes bread crumbs and pastry dough, and it will produce worry-free mayonnaise and other emulsion sauces.

RICH TOMATO SAUCE ♥

This goes really well with pasta, as well as with the beanburgers on page 55, anything grilled on the barbecue, and with vegetarian sausages baked in batter (see page 63).

FOR 6

3 ½ pounds ripe tomatoes, peeled (see page 59), or 2 cans (28 ounces each) tomatoes, drained	*1 can (6 ounces) tomato paste*
	1 tbsp chopped fresh oregano or tarragon
2 tbsp olive oil	*1 tbsp each chopped fresh basil and thyme*
1 large onion, chopped	*sea salt and freshly ground pepper*
2 tbsp chopped garlic	

Cut fresh or canned tomatoes into small cubes. Heat the olive oil and sauté the onion and garlic, stirring, for 1 minute. Add the chopped tomatoes and the tomato paste, then the herbs. Stir well and bring to a simmer. Cook over very low heat, covered, for 20–25 minutes. Season to taste.

LIGHT TOMATO SAUCE ♥

The simplest possible way of making tomato sauce, and beautifully healthy. Use plum-type tomatoes when they are in season; at other times of the year, make the sauce with canned tomatoes.

FOR 2–3

1 can (16 ounces) tomatoes, or 1 pound fresh tomatoes, peeled (see page 59) and chopped	*1 tbsp dried herbes de Provence or dried mixed herbs of your choice*
2 shallots or 4 green onions, minced	*1 large clove garlic, minced*
	sea salt and freshly ground black pepper

Put all the ingredients into the blender and blend until smooth. Season to taste. Heat through gently for 5–6 minutes before serving.

BELOW: (left to right) Hollandaise, Simple Pesto, Rich Tomato and Light Tomato sauces

NO-COOK SALSA ⱽ

So quick and easy to make, this fresh sauce gives the taste buds some vigorous exercise and is indispensable with Mexican food (see pages 33 to 39).

FOR 2–3

4 large tomatoes, peeled (see page 59) and chopped (canned or fresh)	*1 fresh hot chile pepper, sliced*
2 green onions, chopped	*small bunch of fresh cilantro, chopped*

Put the ingredients into the blender and work until smooth. Store in an airtight jar in the refrigerator.

TOMATO AND CHILE SALSA ⱽ

An easy, quickly made sauce, this is lovely with barbecued foods (see pages 119 to 125), and with anything Mexican (see pages 33 to 39).

FOR 2–3

5 tomatoes, peeled (see page 59) and diced	*½ purple or red onion, finely chopped*
juice of 1½ lemons	*sea salt to taste*
1½ cans (4 ounces each) mild green chiles, drained and minced, or fresh hot chiles to taste	*1 tbsp chopped fresh cilantro (optional)*

Mix all the ingredients together and simmer 10–15 minutes over very gentle heat. Season to taste with a little salt and stir in the cilantro, if using.

CHILI SAUCE ⱽ

A full-blooded chili sauce, rich and full of flavor. It is always welcome at a barbecue party. Try it with meatless meatballs (see page 33) or loaf (page 73) as well as with the quesadillas on page 62.

MAKES 2 CUPS

1 sweet onion, finely chopped	*1 can (16 ounces) crushed tomatoes, with juice, or 1 pound fresh tomatoes, peeled (see page 59) and chopped*
1 tbsp olive oil	
1 large clove garlic, minced	
1-2 fresh hot green chile peppers, finely sliced	*juice of ½ lemon*
	sea salt

Soften the onion in the olive oil over low heat, covered with a lid, for 5–6 minutes. Add the garlic and chile and cook for a few minutes longer, until the chile is well softened. Add the tomatoes and heat through for 5 minutes. Finish with the lemon juice, and season to taste with salt. Keep refrigerated in an airtight jar.

Chile Heat

If using fresh chiles, remove the seeds and veins first if you want to control the heat.

BARBECUE SAUCE ♥

The perfect sauce for marinating vegetables before you put them on the barbecue – sharp, and full of flavor. Serve it with barbecued vegetables as well as vegetarian burgers and sausages.

MAKES 2½ CUPS

1¼ cups tomato ketchup	2 heaping tbsp brown sugar
juice of 1 lemon	2 tbsp olive oil
⅔ cup red or white wine vinegar	2 tbsp mild mustard
	2 tbsp sweet pickle relish
6 cloves garlic, minced	

Put the tomato ketchup into a bowl with the lemon juice. Measure the vinegar and pour it into the ketchup bottle; shake well so that you clean the bottle, and add the liquid to the bowl. Mix thoroughly, then stir in the rest of the ingredients and it is ready to use. Keep refrigerated in an airtight jar.

SWEET AND SOUR SAUCE ♥

A classic sauce to go with Chinese egg-fried rice (see page 94) or with steamed or grilled vegetables. You can also toss it into stir-fried vegetables just before serving, and it's indispensable at a barbecue!

MAKES 1¼ CUPS

⅔ cup pineapple juice	1-inch piece fresh gingerroot, peeled and finely grated
3 tbsp olive oil	
¼ cup firmly packed light brown sugar	2 cloves garlic, minced
	¼ cup fresh lemon juice
1 tbsp soy sauce or more to taste	1 heaping tbsp cornstarch
	freshly ground black pepper

Combine the pineapple juice, oil, sugar, soy sauce, gingerroot, garlic, and 2 tbsp of the lemon juice in a saucepan. Heat until the sugar dissolves. Mix the cornstarch with the remaining lemon juice, add to the pan, and stir until the sauce is smooth and thick. Season with pepper. Simmer very gently about 5 minutes, stirring occasionally.

MIXED WILD MUSHROOM SAUCE

The exquisite flavors of wild or Chinese mushrooms in this light, creamy sauce makes it the perfect sauce for pasta. You can also serve it with the rice and vegetable cheese bake on page 100, the mille-feuilles with baby vegetables (page 116), or meatless meatballs (page 73).

FOR 3–4

¾ pound fresh wild or Chinese mushrooms, e.g. cèpes or porcini, chanterelles, shiitake, oyster, etc.	*2 tbsp chopped fresh thyme or 1 tbsp dried thyme*
	1¼ cups crème fraîche or light cream
2 tbsp olive oil	*2 tbsp fresh lemon juice*
sea salt and freshly ground black pepper	

Slice the mushrooms into even lengths. Sauté them in the olive oil until the juices run a little; don't let the mushrooms get too soft. Season to taste with salt and pepper. Add the thyme and stir in. Slowly add the crème fraîche or cream and heat through for 3–4 minutes. Add the lemon juice and check the seasoning.

MEATLESS BOLOGNESE SAUCE ⌄

This famous sauce is easy, and always popular. You can flavor it as you like by adding extra herbs, garlic, or spices to suit the family's tastes. It freezes well and is a useful standby to have.

FOR 4

1 large onion, sliced	*1 tbsp each chopped fresh parsley and chives*
2-3 large cloves garlic, finely sliced	*¼-½ tsp cayenne pepper (optional)*
2 tbsp olive oil	*sea salt and freshly ground black pepper*
¼ pound mushrooms, sliced	
2 cups vegetarian mince	
2 cans (16 ounces each) crushed tomatoes, with juice	

Cook the onion and garlic in the oil over gentle heat, covered with a lid, until quite soft, about 10 minutes. Stir occasionally. Stir in the mushrooms and vegetarian mince and cook, stirring, for 5 minutes. Then add the tomatoes and herbs and simmer until well amalgamated, 5–6 minutes. Season to taste with cayenne, salt, and black pepper.

BÉCHAMEL SAUCE

MAKES 2 CUPS

4 tbsp butter or margarine

3 tbsp flour

2 cups skim or soy milk, warmed

pinch of grated nutmeg

sea salt and freshly ground pepper

Melt the butter in a small, heavy-bottomed saucepan. Gradually stir in the flour, using a wooden spoon. Add the warm milk slowly, stirring all the time until the sauce thickens. Season to taste with nutmeg, salt, and pepper and simmer over very low heat for 5–6 minutes.

For 1¼ cups béchamel, use 3 tbsp butter or margarine, 2 tbsp flour, and 1¼ cups milk.

CHEESE AND PARSLEY SAUCE

This popular sauce goes wonderfully well with the cottage crunch casserole on page 67. Its flavors also complement turnovers (see page 112), a meatless loaf (page 62), and the vegetable strudel on page 110.

MAKES 2 CUPS

3 tbsp margarine

2 tbsp flour

1 tbsp mild mustard

⅔ cup skim or soy milk

½ cup shredded cheddar cheese

medium bunch of parsley, finely chopped

⅔ cup crème fraîche or light cream (or more milk)

freshly ground black pepper

Melt the margarine in a heavy-bottomed saucepan and stir in the flour. When well mixed, stir in the mustard. Slowly add the milk, stirring all the time so that the sauce becomes smooth and thick. Add the shredded cheese and the parsley and cook gently for 5 minutes. Add the cream or extra milk, stir until completely smooth, and season to taste with black pepper.

GRAVY ᵛ

A standby for so many meals, this gravy is wonderful with the meatless meatballs on page 73, the meatless loaf (page 62), with vegetarian sausages, and, of course, dumplings (see page 31).

MAKES 2½ CUPS

1 onion, finely chopped

3 tbsp margarine

1½ cups chopped mushrooms

3-4 tbsp gravy granules

2½ cups boiling water or stock

1-2 tbsp soy sauce or tomato paste

sea salt and freshly ground black pepper

Soften the onion in the margarine for 4–5 minutes over a low heat, covered with a lid. Add the mushrooms and cook until the juices run. Add the gravy granules to the boiling water and stir until thick. Pour onto the vegetables and stir until well amalgamated. Season to taste with soy sauce or tomato paste, and add salt and pepper if necessary.

SPICY CHILI DIP v

*I*f you like the heat of chili, this dip is for you – and it's quite substantial, too. Lovely with corn chips, pita bread, raw mushrooms, and crudités.

FOR 4

¾ cup drained canned tomatoes	½ red bell pepper, seeded and chopped
1 cup drained canned kidney beans	3 green onions, sliced
1 tbsp tomato paste	1 fresh hot red chile pepper, finely sliced
dash of soy sauce	sea salt and freshly ground black pepper
2 large cloves garlic, minced	fresh cilantro for garnish

Put all the prepared ingredients into a blender and blend until smooth. Season to taste, and serve garnished with chopped cilantro.

DILL CUCUMBER DIP

*T*his pale green dip has a lovely summery flavor, and makes light food for hot weather. Serve with potato chips, raw vegetables, or whole-wheat toast, or as a sauce for a main dish.

FOR 4

½ hothouse cucumber, shredded	1-2 tbsp finely chopped onion
	juice of ½ lemon
1¼ cups sour cream	sea salt and freshly ground black pepper
¼ cup chopped fresh dill or 2 tbsp dried dillweed	

Pat the shredded cucumber dry on paper towels. Put all the ingredients in a bowl and mix thoroughly. Put in a serving dish and chill at least 1 hour before serving.

SOUR CREAM ONION DIP

*S*implicity itself, this dip is amazingly delicious and a huge favorite whenever it appears. Serve with tortilla or potato chips and a selection of crudités.

FOR 4-6

1 package dried onion soup mix (approx 30 g)	2 cups sour cream

Stir the dried soup into the sour cream and put into a decorative bowl. Chill 1 hour or so before serving.

REFRIED BEAN DIP

*T*he satisfying flavors and textures of this dip, inspired by Mexican cooking, make it a firm favorite at parties. Taco sauces, in varying heats, make a useful standby on the pantry or refrigerator shelf. Serve the dip with tortilla chips before a meal, at any time of the year.

FOR 4-6

1 cup canned refried beans	4-5 green onions, finely sliced
2-3 tbsp taco sauce	1-2 tsp chili sauce
1 cup shredded cheddar cheese	1 cup crème fraîche or sour cream
	sea salt

Heat the refried beans gently, mashing them with the taco sauce. Stir in the cheese until it melts, then add the green onions and chili relish to taste. Stir in the crème fraîche or sour cream and heat through. Season with salt, and serve warm or cold.

ARTICHOKE DIP

A delicately flavored dip that goes very well on a mixed buffet table. Or hand it around with corn chips or raw carrot and celery sticks, as a nibble before a meal.

FOR 4

½ pound artichoke bottoms, canned or freshly cooked

½ red onion, finely chopped

1 clove garlic, minced

2 tbsp minced parsley

1 tbsp chopped fresh oregano or 1 tsp dried oregano

½ cup grated pecorino romano cheese

⅔ cup bottled or homemade mayonnaise (see page 150)

sea salt and freshly ground black pepper

Put all the ingredients into a blender and blend until smooth. Season to taste and chill.

GUACAMOLE ᴠ

T here are endless versions of this famous Mexican avocado dip: here is mine! Serve with tortilla chips or pita bread, or with raw mushrooms, celery, carrots, and other crudités of your choice.

FOR 4–6

2 tomatoes, peeled (see page 59) and chopped

juice of 2 large lemons

1 fresh hot red chile pepper, very finely sliced, or 1 can (4 ounces) mild green chiles, drained and finely chopped

2 cloves garlic, finely sliced (optional)

4 green onions, finely sliced (optional)

2 large avocados, mashed

sea salt and freshly ground black pepper

Combine all the ingredients except the avocado in the food processor and work until very smooth. Stir in the avocado with a fork and season to taste.

GREEN HERB DIP

S uperb for a summer party, fresh, aromatic herbs give their wonderful qualities to this creamy green dip. Serve it with raw vegetables to scoop it up, tortilla chips, and strips of pita bread. Lovely with drinks before a meal, or as part of a buffet table. It also makes a great pasta sauce.

FOR 6–8

¼ cup chopped parsley

¼ cup chopped fresh dill

bunch of watercress, chopped

3 green onions, finely sliced

1 cup cooked, drained spinach, squeezed dry

1¼ cups bottled or homemade mayonnaise (see page 150)

1¼ cups sour cream

sea salt and freshly ground black pepper

small pinch of paprika

Put the chopped parsley, dill, and watercress into the food processor and blend until they are minced. Turn into a bowl and add the green onions. Blend the cooked spinach until very smooth. Add to the herbs and stir in the mayonnaise. Mix thoroughly, then stir in the sour cream. Season to taste with salt, pepper, and paprika and chill before serving.

CHAPTER NINE

Desserts, Cakes and Cookies

Very few people can resist a really delicious dessert or slice of cake, even when they think they should. But judicious amounts of something sweet at regular intervals are not such a bad thing for the general health!

The irresistible factor of a tiramisù or a pecan pie is undeniable, and desserts like this can grace the table at any time of the year. Crème brûlée, sticky toffee pudding, and luscious chocolate desserts are everybody's favorites, ideal for all seasons. Fruit desserts are well-loved, too. Fruit salads and sorbets make good use of fragrant soft fruits in summer, but autumn is the time when fruits really come into their own, with crisp apples, blackberries, and blueberries as well as fresh nuts. You can freeze some of this produce – apples in the form of a purée, or berries just as they are. Then, in the chill depths of winter or early spring, you can produce an exquisite pie, tart, or cheesecake from the contents of the freezer.

Classic cakes – lemon, chocolate, carrot, and mixed fruit – and cookies are also a part of the pleasures of home cooking and family life.

CHOCOLATE MOUSSE

A divinely rich dessert that shows why chocolate mousse is such a universal favorite! For the best flavor, use a good-quality bittersweet chocolate.

FOR 4–6

4 ounces dark chocolate, broken into small pieces	1 cup heavy cream or crème fraîche
3 jumbo free-range eggs, separated	3 tbsp superfine sugar
1 ½ tbsp water	whipped cream and grated chocolate to decorate
2 tbsp sweet liqueur such as Chartreuse, Amaretto, or Grand Marnier	

Put the chocolate in a small heatproof bowl and set in a pan of hot water to melt. Alternatively, melt in the microwave. Set aside to cool slightly.

Combine the egg yolks and water in a large heatproof bowl and set over a pan of simmering water. Whisk for a minute or so until the yolks start to thicken, being extremely careful not to let them curdle. Add the liqueur and continue whisking until the mixture is pale, very thick, and increased in volume. Remove from the heat.

Add the melted chocolate to the whisked mixture and fold it in gently but thoroughly.

Whip the cream or crème fraîche until it starts to thicken. Add 1 tbsp of the sugar and continue whipping until thick. Fold into the chocolate mixture.

In a clean bowl, beat the egg whites until soft peaks will form. Add the remaining sugar and continue beating until stiff. Fold the egg whites into the chocolate mixture.

Spoon the mousse into a serving bowl or individual ramekins. Cover and chill. When ready to serve, decorate with whipped cream and grated chocolate.

FROZEN VANILLA MOUSSE

This mousse is like a simple ice cream made without a custard. The mousse can also be made with Greek yogurt, rather than cream, and sweetened with honey instead of sugar. You can stir a little stewed fresh or dried fruit or chopped nuts into the cream mixture before folding in the egg white, to vary the flavor.

FOR 3–4

1 cup heavy cream	1 free-range egg white
¼ cup confectioners' sugar, sifted	¼ tsp salt
½ tsp vanilla extract	

Whip the cream until it starts to thicken. Add the confectioners' sugar and vanilla and continue whipping until the cream is thick.

In another bowl, beat the egg white with the salt until stiff. Fold the egg white into the cream mixture. Spoon into a mold or ice-cube tray, cover, and freeze without stirring.

Serve with a sauce or with crushed soft fruits.

RASPBERRY MOUSSE

This basic fruit mousse can be endlessly varied, using other fruits (in season or frozen) with their matching gelatin or a contrasting flavor. Vegetarian fruit gelatins use agar agar, made from seaweed, as the setting agent, rather than gelatin (which is derived from animals).

FOR 4

1 pkg vegetarian raspberry gelatin

1¼ cups heavy cream

2 cups fresh or thawed frozen raspberries

whipped cream and chopped nuts to decorate

Make the fruit gelatin as directed on the package. Let it cool but not set.

Whip the cream. Whip the fruit gelatin and fold in the whipped cream. Fold in the fruit. Pour into a dish or mold and chill until set.

Serve in the dish, or unmolded, decorated with whipped cream and chopped nuts.

Since vegetarian gelatin sets less hard than regular gelatin, some separation may occur. If this happens, mix the mousse up again and serve in the dish, decorated as above.

FRUIT SORBET

A refreshing fruit sorbet is the perfect dessert in hot weather. You can make it sweet or a little tart, according to your taste. If you don't have an ice-cream machine, you can freeze the sorbet in an ice-cube tray, whisking it two or three times to break up ice crystals.

FOR 6

1½ pounds fresh or frozen raspberries, strawberries, or other fruit of your choice

about ⅔ cup sugar

¼ cup water

juice of 1 lemon

Purée the fruit in a blender or food processor. If it has small seeds (as raspberries do), press the purée through a strainer.

Combine the sugar and water in a saucepan and heat, stirring to dissolve the sugar. Bring to a boil and boil the syrup until it reaches 230°F on a candy thermometer. Remove from the heat and let cool.

When the syrup is cold, mix it with the fruit purée and stir in the lemon juice. Taste the mixture and add more sugar or lemon juice if liked: the flavor should be quite strong.

Pour into an ice-cream machine and freeze until firm.

OPPOSITE: Raspberry Mousse (large dish) and Raspberry Sorbet

BAKED CHOCOLATE PUDDING WITH FUDGE SAUCE

Who can resist this combination, the chocolate cake smelling so good in the oven and served warm, soaked in fudge sauce. A real family favorite.

FOR 6

¾ cup (6 ounces) margarine	1 tsp vanilla extract
¾ cup firmly packed light brown sugar	
1¼ cups all-purpose flour	For the fudge sauce:
½ cup whole-wheat flour	¾ cup firmly packed light brown sugar
⅔ cup unsweetened cocoa	
1 tbsp baking powder	1 cup light cream
4 free-range eggs, beaten	2 tbsp margarine

Cream the margarine with the sugar until light and fluffy. Sift the flours with the cocoa and baking powder (tip the bran from the sifter into the mixture). Beat the flour mixture into the creamed mixture alternately with the eggs, beating until light. Add the vanilla. Turn into an 8-inch round ovenproof dish and bake in a preheated 375°F oven until a sharp knife inserted in the center comes out clean, 40–45 minutes.

Meanwhile, make the sauce: Put the sugar, cream, and margarine into a heavy-bottomed saucepan. Bring to a boil, stirring to dissolve the sugar, then turn the heat down until the mixture is simmering and cook until it is thick, about 5 minutes.

Pour the sauce over the hot pudding and let stand up to an hour or so before eating, so that the cake has a chance to soak up the sauce.

TIRAMISÙ

This is an absolutely brilliant version of a world-famous dessert – slightly less rich than some recipes, but full of that coffee flavor, and well laced with brandy!

FOR 4–6

⅔ cup strong black coffee	½ cup ricotta cheese
2 tbsp brandy	½ cup sugar
6 ounces ladyfingers	1 tsp vanilla extract
1 cup (½ pound) mascarpone or cream cheese	3 free-range egg whites
½ cup plain yogurt	1-2 tbsp grated chocolate

Mix the coffee with the brandy in a shallow dish. Dip half of the ladyfingers very briefly into the mixture to moisten them, then use to line the bottom of a glass bowl. Mix together the mascarpone, yogurt, and ricotta until smooth, and add the sugar and vanilla. Beat the egg whites until stiff, and fold into the cheese mixture. Spoon half of this over the layer of ladyfingers. Make a second layer of moistened ladyfingers and cover with the rest of the cheese mixture. Sprinkle grated chocolate on top, cover, and chill several hours before serving.

CHOCOLATE DELIGHT

This sumptuous dessert of sherry-moistened sponge cake surrounding a rich chocolate-mousse filling, all covered with whipped cream, is always a huge success. Everyone always asks for the recipe, so here it is!

FOR 8–10

1 ¼ cups milk	*6 free-range eggs, separated*
dash of sherry	*8 ounces semisweet chocolate*
8 thin slices of plain cake	*1¼ cups heavy cream,*
¾ cup (6 ounces) margarine	*whipped*
½ cup sugar	*grated chocolate for decoration*
pinch of salt	

Mix the milk with the sherry in a shallow dish. Dip the slices of cake in it briefly to moisten, then use to line a greased 8-inch soufflé dish. Line the sides first and then cover the bottom.

Cream the margarine with the sugar and salt until light and fluffy, then beat in the egg yolks. Beat until the mixture is pale yellow. Melt the chocolate in a bowl over hot water, or in the microwave. Gradually beat the chocolate into the egg yolk mixture. In another bowl, beat the egg whites until very stiff, and fold into the mixture. Pour into the cake-lined dish, cover, and chill at least 24 hours.

CRÈME BRÛLÉE

This is a healthy version of a famous classic, using crème fraîche instead of heavy cream. To vary it, put halved seeded grapes or red currants, or sliced banana or pear, in the bottom of each ramekin before pouring in the custard.

FOR 6

2½ cups crème fraîche	*¼ cup granulated sugar*
thinly pared rind of 1 lemon,	*a few drops of vanilla extract*
cut in thin strips	*6 heaping tbsp light brown*
4 egg yolks from jumbo free-	*sugar*
range eggs	

Simmer the crème fraîche with the lemon rind gently for 10 minutes. Let cool 10 minutes. Beat the egg yolks with the granulated sugar in a heatproof bowl until pale and creamy, add the vanilla extract, then strain in the crème fraîche, stirring well. Place the bowl over a pan of hot – not boiling – water and cook until the custard thickens, 20–25 minutes, stirring occasionally. Don't let the water come to boiling point at any stage. When ready, the custard will be velvety in consistency and will lightly coat the back of a spoon. Put into 6 ramekin dishes and chill overnight.

The next day, sprinkle 1 heaping tbsp light brown sugar over the top of each custard and smooth evenly. Place under a very hot broiler until the sugar has melted and is bubbling, 3–4 minutes. Let cool, then chill again up to 8 hours.

NEXT SPREAD: (left to right) Crème Brûlée, Redcurrant Cheesecake, Chocolate Delight, and Pecan Pie

REDCURRANT CHEESECAKE

A very easy uncooked cheesecake, this is simply fresh redcurrants folded into cheese and whipped cream, on a crunchy base. Other soft fruits in season, such as raspberries, sliced black currants, strawberries, and blueberries, can be used instead of redcurrants.

FOR 6–8

2 cups graham-cracker crumbs	*1¼ cups heavy cream, whipped*
4 tbsp margarine, melted	*½ pound redcurrants, topped and tailed*
4 cups (2 pounds) cream cheese	
1 cup firmly packed light brown sugar	

Combine the graham-cracker crumbs and melted margarine and mix thoroughly. Press evenly over the bottom of a greased 8-inch loose-bottomed tart pan. Chill until set.

Beat the cream cheese with the sugar until creamy. Fold in the whipped cream, then carefully fold in the redcurrants. Pile onto the prepared base and smooth the surface. Chill several hours, or overnight, before serving.

PECAN PIE

A great American classic, this recipe brings out the best in a delicious nut. Serve the pie warm or at room temperature, with whipped cream or ice cream.

FOR 6

½ recipe quantity sweet piecrust dough (see page 179)	*⅔ cup light corn syrup*
4 tbsp margarine	*⅓ cup skim milk*
½ cup firmly packed light brown sugar	*1 tsp vanilla extract*
2 free-range eggs, beaten	*1½ cups pecan halves*
1 tbsp flour	

Roll out the piecrust dough and line an 8-inch loose-bottomed tart pan. Bake blind until part cooked (see page 115).

Cream the margarine with the sugar until light and fluffy, then beat in the eggs. Beat in the flour, syrup, and milk. Add the vanilla and beat thoroughly until the mixture is light.

Arrange the nuts on the bottom of the pastry shell and pour the syrup mixture over them. Bake in a preheated 375°F oven for 15 minutes, then turn the heat down to 325°F and continue baking until a knife inserted in the center comes out clean, about 30 minutes longer. Serve warm or cold.

166

LEMON SOUFFLÉ TART

A party piece, this is complicated to make but a stunning finale to a special meal. It is intensely lemony, incredibly light, and needs only a little cream to go with it.

FOR 12

⅔ recipe quantity sweet piecrust dough (see page 179)	⅔ cup fresh lemon juice
	4 tbsp margarine
4 jumbo free-range eggs, separated	pinch of salt
1 ¼ cups granulated sugar	3 tbsp confectioners' sugar

Roll out the piecrust dough and line an 11-inch loose-bottomed tart pan. Bake blind (see page 115) in a preheated 425°F oven for 15 minutes, then uncover and bake 5 minutes longer. Let cool on a wine rack.

Beat the egg yolks with half of the granulated sugar until thick and pale, then stir in the lemon juice. Put into a heavy-bottomed saucepan and heat gently, gradually adding the margarine. Stir constantly, being careful not to overheat to simmering point, until the mixture thickens. Let cool, then chill 1–2 hours.

Beat the egg whites with the salt until they form soft peaks. Beat in the remaining granulated sugar 1 tbsp at a time and continue beating until the mixture is stiff and glossy.

Fold one-quarter of the egg whites into the lemon mixture, then carefully fold in the rest. Pour into the baked pastry shell and bake in a preheated 375°F oven until the filling is puffed and light golden brown, about 15 minutes. Let cool on a wire rack at least 1 hour.

Just before serving sift the confectioners' sugar over the top.

BAKEWELL TART

One of the great traditional recipes of England, this tart consistently lives up to its excellent reputation. Serve it warm or at room temperature.

FOR 8

1 recipe quantity sweet piecrust dough (see page 179)	1 cup sugar
	2⅔ cups ground almonds
⅓ cup raspberry jam	3 tbsp all-purpose flour
1 cup (½ pound) margarine	4 free-range eggs, beaten

Roll out the piecrust dough and line a 12-inch loose-bottomed tart pan. Spread the jam evenly over the bottom. Cream the margarine with the sugar until light and fluffy, then beat in the almonds and add the sifted flour. Beat in the eggs until the mixture is light and smooth. Pour into the pastry shell and spread it out.

Bake in a preheated 375°F oven for 45 minutes, watching toward the end in case it darkens too much. (You can cover the top with a piece of foil if it begins to burn.) Let cool on a wire rack.

PEACH OR PLUM COBBLER

A fruit cobbler epitomizes the best of home cooking. You can use other fruits besides peaches or plums – apples, pears, and so on. It is a great American classic dessert.

FOR 6

2 pounds ripe peaches, skinned, or plums, pits removed

2-3 tbsp sugar

1 tsp grated lemon rind

1 tbsp fresh lemon juice

For the cobbler topping:

1 ¼ cups all-purpose flour

pinch of salt

2 tbsp sugar

1 tsp baking powder

3 tbsp margarine

1 free-range egg, beaten

2-4 tbsp skim milk or light cream

Slice the pitted fruit and put it in a baking dish with sugar to taste and the lemon rind and juice.

To make the topping, sift the dry ingredients into a bowl and cut in the margarine until it resembles fine bread crumbs. Fold in the beaten egg and then enough milk or cream to bind to a light dough. Knead for a few moments. Divide the dough into 8 portions and shape each into a flat patty. Place them over the top of the fruit. Bake in a preheated 400°F oven until the cobbler topping is golden brown, 25–30 minutes.

Serve warm, with whipped cream or ice cream.

> ### Skinning Peaches
> Put peaches into a large bowl and cover with boiling water. Leave to stand for about 2 minutes. Lift out one by one and pierce the kin with a sharp knife; the skin will peel off easily.

BLUEBERRY TART

Here, a sweet almond piecrust holds a rich blueberry filling topped with sweetened yogurt. The blueberries aren't cooked so they keep their shape as well as their vitamins. If you prefer, you can make a more traditional blueberry pie following the recipe for apple pie on page 170.

FOR 6

¾ recipe quantity Austrian piecrust dough (see page 179)

1 cup granulated sugar

¼ cup cornstarch

pinch of salt

1 ¼ cups water

2 pounds (about 3 cups) blueberries

3-4 tbsp confectioners' sugar

1 cup thick plain yogurt

Roll out the piecrust dough and line a 9-inch pie pan, pressing in the dough evenly with your knuckles. Bake blind (see page 115) in a preheated 375°F oven for 20 minutes, then uncover and crisp up for 5 minutes longer. Let cool.

Mix together the sugar, cornstarch, salt, and water in a saucepan and heat gently, stirring, until thick and smooth. Simmer gently 5 minutes. Add half of the blueberries at a time and mix thoroughly. Let cool. Just before serving, pour the blueberry mixture into the cooked pastry shell. Sift the confectioners' sugar into the yogurt, stir well, and spoon over the top of the tart.

OPPOSITE: Plum Cobbler

APPLE SPONGE PUDDING

*H*ere, tender sugar-glazed apples are baked on a sweet sponge batter base – an ideal dessert for a chilly day. Serve hot or at room temperature, with whipped cream.

FOR 4–6

⅔ cup sugar	*¾ cup all-purpose flour*
1 jumbo free-range egg	*1 ½ tsp baking powder*
4 tbsp margarine	*½ tsp ground cloves (optional)*
⅓ cup skim or soy milk	*¾ pound tart apples*
	lemon juice

Reserve 1½ tbsp of the sugar; put the remaining sugar in a bowl with the egg and whisk until thick and creamy. Heat the margarine and milk in a saucepan and bring to a boil. Pour into the egg and sugar mixture, whisking. Sift together the flour, baking powder, and optional cloves and fold into the egg mixture, making sure there are no lumps of flour. Pour the batter into a greased 6- x 9-inch baking pan.

Peel and core the apples and cut into slices. Arrange on top of the sponge batter, leaving no gaps. Sprinkle with lemon juice and then with the reserved sugar. Bake in a preheated 400°F oven until well risen and golden brown, about 40 minutes.

Serve hot or let cool before serving in slices.

APPLE PIE

*T*he best apple pies are made with the autumn varieties of tart apples that keep their shape. But this pie is a treat at any time of the year, made with whatever apples that are in season. Serve with thick yogurt or ice cream.

FOR 4–6

1 recipe quantity sweet piecrust dough (see page 179)	*¼-½ cup sugar*
⅔ cup ground almonds	*3 whole cloves*
1 ½ pounds apples, peeled and cored	*2 tbsp margarine*
	beaten free-range egg for glazing

Butter a 9- to 10-inch fluted tart dish or pie pan. Roll out half of the piecrust dough and line the dish. Sprinkle with the ground almonds - they mop up the juices and prevent the pastry from going soggy. Slice the apples very thinly in the food processor and arrange in the pie shell, sprinkling with sugar to taste as you go. Tuck the cloves into the fruit and dot with the margarine.

Moisten the edge of the pie shell. Roll out the rest of the piecrust dough and lay over the top. Press the edges together with a fork to seal them. Trim. Make a few slits in the top crust and brush with beaten egg.

Bake in a preheated 425°F oven until the pastry is lightly browned, 30–35 minutes. Serve hot or cold.

SPONGE PUDDING WITH APRICOTS AND ALMONDS

One of the simplest recipes ever, this is a family favorite at any time of year. If fresh apricots aren't in season, you can substitute canned apricot halves or dried apricots that have been soaked until plump and tender. Other fruits can replace the apricots: plums, peaches, nectarines, and bananas, for example.

FOR 3-4

¾ pound ripe but firm apricots, halved and pits removed	⅓ cup firmly packed light brown sugar
	1 jumbo free-range egg
For the sponge topping:	½ tsp vanilla extract
½ cup self-rising flour	milk if needed
4 tbsp margarine	⅓ cup sliced almonds, toasted and roughly chopped

To make the sponge topping, sift the flour into a bowl and add the margarine, sugar, egg, and vanilla. Beat together until light and creamy. If the mixture seems a little dry, add a small amount of milk. Stir in the almonds.

Arrange the apricots in a 3-cup baking dish and cover with the sponge topping. Bake in a preheated 325°F oven until the topping is well risen and golden brown, 30–35 minutes. Serve hot, with cream or ice cream.

The Electric Mixer

This is indispensable for making cakes and biscuits, as well ass many desserts. It beats air into a mixture in a way that even the strongest of wrists cannot!

FLOATING ISLANDS

No one can resist this dessert of tender poached meringue "islands" floating on a custard "sea." The custard is stabilized with cornstarch, which will prevent any curdling.

FOR 6-8

1 quart milk	½ tsp vanilla or almond extract, or ¼ tsp apple pie spice
3 free-range eggs, separated	
⅔ cup superfine sugar	
1 tbsp cornstarch	raspberry jelly
½ tsp salt	

Heat the milk in a wide saucepan. Meanwhile, put 2 of the egg whites in a bowl and beat until frothy. Add 2 tbsp of the sugar and beat until stiff.

Drop large heaping spoonfuls of the egg whites onto the hot milk, to make 6 or 8 meringues. Poach gently until the meringues feel just firm to the touch, turning them over so that they are cooked on both sides. When they are ready, remove with a slotted spoon and drain on paper towels.

Combine the remaining sugar, cornstarch, and salt in a bowl and stir to mix. Add the remaining egg white and the egg yolks and mix together until smoothly blended. Pour in the hot milk, stirring. Pour the custard mixture into the top of a double boiler set over simmering water, or into a heavy-based saucepan, and cook until thickened, stirring constantly. Remove from the heat and cool slightly, then stir in the extract or spice. Pour the custard into a wide serving dish and let cool completely.

Before serving, arrange the meringues on top of the custard and dot with raspberry jelly.

CARROT CAKE WITH CREAM CHEESE FROSTING

This rich carrot cake is made with cooked puréed carrots, which makes it deliciously moist, and it has some coconut and walnuts in it as well to add texture. Wonderful at teatime, and also as a dessert.

FOR 10–12

1 ²⁄₃ cups all-purpose flour	1 pound carrots, cooked and puréed (about 2 cups)
1 cup firmly packed light brown sugar	1 cup chopped walnuts
pinch of salt	²⁄₃ cup dried shredded coconut
1 tsp baking powder	For the cream cheese frosting:
2 tsp ground cinnamon	
³⁄₄ cup sunflower oil	1 cup (½ pound) low-fat cream cheese
2 free-range eggs, lightly beaten	2 cups confectioners' sugar
1 tsp vanilla extract	1 tbsp fresh lemon juice

Sift the dry ingredients into a bowl. Add the oil, eggs, and vanilla and beat well. The mixture will be quite sticky. Beat in the carrots, mixing thoroughly. Fold in the walnuts and coconut.

Pour into a greased 8-inch cake pan and bake in a preheated 350°F oven until a sharp knife inserted into the center comes out clean, about 1¼ hours. Let cool on a rack.

To make the cream cheese frosting, mash the cheese and slowly sift in the confectioners' sugar, beating until fully incorporated. Stir in the lemon juice.

When the cake is cold, cut it into two layers and fill with one-third of the cream cheese frosting. Spread the remaining frosting over the top and sides of the cake.

VEGAN FRUIT CAKE ♥

This rich, dark, moist cake contains no sugar, just a little corn syrup, relying instead on the natural sweetness of the dried fruits and fruit juice. Wrapped tightly and stored in an airtight tin, the cake will keep very well.

MAKES A 9½- X 6-INCH CAKE

2 cups golden raisins	7 tbsp margarine
1½ cups currants	2 cups unsweetened fruit juice
2⅓ cups candied cherries, halved	1 cup soy milk
1 cup raisins, chopped	2 cups whole-wheat flour
2 tbsp chopped candied ginger (optional)	2 cups whole-wheat self-rising flour
¼ cup light corn syrup	2 tsp apple pie spice

Combine the fruits, corn syrup, margarine, and fruit juice in a large saucepan. Stir over low heat until the margarine has melted, then cover the pan and simmer for 5 minutes. Pour the fruit mixture into a large bowl and let cool to room temperature.

Add the soy milk and stir to mix. Sift the flours and spice into the bowl (tip in the bran left in the sifter) and mix thoroughly.

Pour the cake batter into a greased and lined 9½- x 6-inch rectangular cake pan and bake in a preheated 325°F oven until a skewer inserted into the center comes out clean, about 3 hours. Let cool, in the pan, on a wire rack.

OPPOSITE: Carrot Cake with Cream Cheese Frosting

LEMON DRIZZLE CAKE

*L*ight but very moist, this lemony cake is perfect for special occasions. It's a popular birthday cake when covered with the cream cheese frosting on page 172.

MAKES 9- X 5-INCH LOAF CAKE

½ cup (4 ounces) margarine	*1 ¼ cups all-purpose flour*
1 cup sugar	*2 tsp baking powder*
finely grated rind and juice of 3 lemons	*⅓ cup skim milk*
2 jumbo free-range eggs, beaten	

Cream the margarine with ¾ cup of the sugar, the lemon rind, and 1 ½ tbsp of the lemon juice until light and fluffy. Beat in the eggs one at a time. Beat in the sifted flour and baking powder, then add the milk. Beat thoroughly until light. Put into a greased 9- x 5-inch loaf pan and bake in a preheated 350°F oven for 45 minutes.

Toward the end of the baking time, heat the remaining lemon juice and sugar until the sugar dissolves. Simmer 3–4 minutes.

Cool the cake, in the pan, on a rack for 5 minutes, then unmold, upside down. Pierce the base of the cake all over with a skewer, being careful not to break through the top surface of the cake. Spoon the lemon syrup carefully over the base of the cake until all of it has been absorbed. Let cool completely before turning the cake right side up.

CHOCOLATE SPONGE CAKE WITH CHOCOLATE BUTTER FROSTING

*T*his light chocolate cake filled and covered with chocolate butter frosting never fails to please.

FOR 8

¾ cup all-purpose flour	For the chocolate butter frosting:
2 tsp baking powder	
3 tbsp unsweetened cocoa powder	*6 tbsp margarine*
½ cup sugar	*3 cups confectioners' sugar, frosting:*
½ cup (4 ounces) margarine	*1 tbsp unsweetened cocoa powder*
2 free-range eggs	
1 tsp vanilla extract	*1-2 tbsp strong black coffee*
	1 ½ ounces semisweet chocolate, grated

Sift the flour, baking powder, and cocoa powder into a large bowl. Add the sugar. Cut in the margarine until it resembles fine bread crumbs. Beat in the eggs, beating until the mixture is very light. Add the vanilla and beat again.

Put the batter into a greased 8-inch round springform cake pan. Bake in a preheated 325°F oven for 30 minutes. Let cool in the pan for a couple of minutes, then carefully unmold onto a wire rack to cool completely.

To make the frosting, cream the margarine with the sifted confectioners' sugar and cocoa until well blended. Add enough coffee to make a spreadable consistency, then fold in the grated chocolate.

When the cake is cold, cut it into two layers and fill with one-third of the chocolate butter frosting. Cover the top and sides of the cake with the remaining frosting.

OPPOSITE: Lemon Drizzle Cake

CRISPY GINGER SNAPS ❦

These gingery cookies have some crystallized ginger in them, which gives a touch of softness in contrast to the crisp bite. They freeze perfectly.

MAKES 18

⅔ cup self-rising flour	*6 tbsp margarine*
¾ cup whole-wheat flour	*3 tbsp sugar*
2½ tsp baking powder	*2 tbsp light corn syrup, heated gently*
½ tsp baking soda	
1½ tsp ground cinnamon	*⅓ cup diced crystallized ginger*
1 tbsp ground ginger	

Sift the dry ingredients into a bowl (tip in the bran left in the sifter). Cut in the margarine until it resembles fine bread crumbs. Mix in the sugar, then the warmed corn syrup and the crystallized ginger. Knead to a light dough.

Break off small pieces of dough the size of a walnut, shape into balls, and put onto a greased baking sheet. Flatten the balls with a fork. Bake in a preheated 400°F oven for 12 minutes. Let cool on the baking sheet for 5 minutes, then lift carefully onto a rack to cool completely.

CHOCOLATE CHIP COOKIES

These ever-popular cookies have the richness of chocolate and the crunch of nuts. Pecans have been suggested, although you could also use walnuts or hazelnuts. They freeze extremely well.

MAKES 10 LARGE OR 15 MEDIUM

½ cup (4 ounces) margarine	*1⅔ cups all-purpose flour*
¼ cup granulated sugar	*1 tsp baking powder*
½ cup firmly packed light brown sugar	*½ tsp salt*
1 free-range egg, beaten	*1 cup chocolate chips*
1 tsp vanilla extract	*1 cup roughly chopped pecans*

Cream the margarine with both of the sugars until light and fluffy. Beat in the egg. Add the vanilla. Sift the flour with the baking powder and salt, and sift again into the bowl. Beat well to mix. Fold in the chocolate chips and the nuts.

Drop spoonfuls of the dough onto a well-greased baking sheet, leaving space around each to allow for spreading. Bake in a preheated 375°F oven until lightly browned, about 15 minutes. Let cool on the baking sheet for 5 minutes before lifting carefully onto a rack to cool completely.

OATMEAL AND RAISIN COOKIES

Great family favorites, these are spiced with a hint of cinnamon. They are delicious with a glass of milk or juice or with a cup of tea or coffee.

MAKES 10

4 tbsp margarine	½ tsp salt
½ cup firmly packed light brown sugar	½ tsp baking powder
	1 tsp ground cinnamon
1 free-range egg	2 cups rolled oats
1 tsp vanilla extract	¾ cup raisins
6 tbsp all-purpose flour	

Cream the margarine with the sugar until light and fluffy. Beat in the egg. Add the vanilla. Sift the flour with the salt, baking powder, and cinnamon, then beat into the egg mixture. Add the oats and raisins and mix thoroughly together.

Drop spoonfuls of dough onto a well-greased baking sheet, leaving space around each to allow for spreading. Bake in a preheated 350°F oven for 15 minutes. Let cool on the baking sheet for 5 minutes, then lift carefully onto a rack to cool completely.

ABOVE: (left to right) Chocolate Chip Cookies, Crispy Ginger Snaps, Oatmeal and Raisin Cookies

CHAPTER TEN

Pastry Basics

FLAKY PASTRY ˅

MAKES 14 OUNCES

1²⁄₃ cups all-purpose flour	¾ cup (6 ounces) margarine
pinch of salt	4-6 tbsp cold water

Sift the flour with the salt into a bowl and cut in ¼ cup of the margarine. Add enough water to bind lightly. Turn onto a floured board and knead until smooth.

Roll out into an oblong. Cover the top of the dough with half of the remaining margarine, in small bits, then fold the dough in three (the bottom third up and the top third down). Moisten the side edges with water and press to seal. Give the dough a quarter turn so that these edges are at the top and bottom. Roll out again into an oblong and repeat the process, using the remaining margarine. Chill 10–15 minutes, then roll out and fold in three once more. The dough is now ready to use as required. Bake at 425°F.

PUFF PASTRY ˅

MAKES 1 POUND

1 ²⁄₃ cups all-purpose flour	²⁄₃ cup ice-cold water
pinch of salt	squeeze of fresh lemon juice
1 cup (½ pound) margarine	

Sift the flour with the salt into a bowl and cut in a walnut-size piece of margarine. Bind with the water and lemon juice and knead to make a smooth dough. Chill 15 minutes.

Roll out the dough to an oblong. Place the margarine, in a block, in the center. Wrap the dough around the margarine like a parcel and turn over. **Roll out to an oblong again, fold in three (the bottom third up and the top third down), and press the side edges to seal them. Give the dough a quarter turn so that these edges are at the top and bottom.** Repeat from ** to **. Wrap in wax paper or a dish towel and chill 15 minutes. Repeat from ** to ** six more times, chilling between each of these "turns." Chill 10 minutes before rolling out finally for baking.

Bake puff pastry at 425°F.

EASY PIECRUST ❧

MAKES 9 OUNCES

6 tbsp margarine	1 cup + 2 tbsp all-purpose flour
⅛ tsp fine sea salt	
	3 tbsp cold water

Put all the ingredients into a blender or food processor and blend until amalgamated and crumbly. Knead to a smooth dough on a floured board, then chill at least 30 minutes before using.

If you don't have a blender or food processor, sift the flour with the salt into a bowl and cut in the margarine, lifting the mixture to incorporate as much air as possible. When the mixture resembles fine bread crumbs, bind with the water. Knead on a floured board until smooth.

AUSTRIAN PIECRUST

MAKES 1 POUND

10 tbsp (5 ounces) margarine	1 cup ground almonds
1 cup all-purpose flour	1 free-range egg yolk
7 tbsp sugar	1 tsp grated lemon rind

Cut the margarine lightly into the sifted flour until the mixture resembles fine bread crumbs. Stir in the sugar and ground almonds. Mix in the egg yolk and lemon rind and knead on a lightly floured board until smooth. Chill 30 minutes. When using, roll out to ¼-inch thickness.

SWEET PIECRUST ❧

MAKES ¾ POUND

1 ⅔ cups all-purpose flour	½ cup (4 ounces) margarine
1 tbsp sugar	3 tbsp cold water

Sift the flour into a large bowl and stir in the sugar. Cut in the margarine lightly until the mixture resembles fine bread crumbs. Bind with the water. Knead lightly on a floured board until smooth. Wrap and chill at least 30 minutes before rolling out.

Vegetarian Questions and Answers

Q What is a vegetarian and what is a vegan?

A A vegetarian is someone who doesn't eat meat, fish, poultry; or any animal. Vegetarians don't eat any foods containing the by-products of slaughter such as gelatin (which is ground-up bones, hooves, hides, etc.), animal rennet (which is prepared from the stomach lining of calves and used in the making of many non-vegetarian cheeses), or lard or suet (the hard waxy fat from the kidneys and loins of sheep and cattle).

A vegetarian diet is based on the foods of the fields – grains, legumes, nuts, seeds, vegetables, and fruit – as is a vegan diet. The difference between vegetarians and vegans is that veggies eat eggs, cheese and other dairy products, whereas vegans eat none of these.

Q What are the reasons for not eating meat?

A For me, the main reason has always been my love of animals. Because of that love, I don't want any animal to die for my plate.

A lot of people who turn vegetarian feel the same – factory-farming methods appall them, as do the way that animals are slaughtered and the way they are transported to their slaughter.

Others are rightfully wary of the large doses of hormones and antibiotics that are pumped into many animals, and wary, too, of the effects of the pesticides that are used on animal feed.

The other big reason for not eating meat is health. More and more surveys suggest that a vegetarian diet can help reduce your risk of cancer, heart disease, diabetes, high blood pressure, and other illnesses. This is partly because vegetarian meals tend to be lower in fat and also because there is no cholesterol in vegetables – only food from animals contains cholesterol.

There's also the matter of the health of the planet to think about. This earth needs all the trees it can get in order to breathe properly, and yet millions of acres are hacked down to clear grazing for cattle and sheep. Many people are now finding it unacceptable that, in order to bring beef to their plates, a huge acreage of Central and South American rainforest has been cleared to provide grazing land for cattle. At a time when treecover of this earth is reducing rapidly, kids need to know that for every quarterpounder made from Central or South American beef, six square yards of rainforest are hewn for pasture.

As the inheritors of the planet, our children also need to know that they and their children will be facing the prospect of a dramatic decline in fresh-water tables principally because of the billions of gallons used each year to rear livestock. For instance, 70 percent of all fresh American water is used in agriculture, and whereas it takes 25 gallons of that water to produce a pound of wheat, it takes an astonishing 5,214 gallons to produce a pound of beef! (Source: University of California)

Q Is a meatless diet a healthy diet?

A Absolutely. It's balanced, it's nutritious; and you're getting the goodness direct from the vegetables and fruit instead of via an animal. Also, as I've said, because it is lower in saturated fat and cholesterol, there are fewer worries about your heart and your weight. Not only is this way of eating healthy, another advantage is that you'll *feel* healthier because your body is not working overtime trying to digest all that meat. You don't feel sluggish, you've got much more get up and go.

Q Will I get enough protein if I don't eat meat?

A Yes, more than enough. It's one of the great myths that vegetarians don't get enough protein from their food. The opposite is the case, even for children – we tend to eat *too much* protein. A balanced diet of fresh vegetables, fruit, nuts, and legumes will provide your daily protein needs.

Q What IS a healthy diet?

A One that keeps you well. Generally speaking, a healthy diet should be low in saturated fats, low in

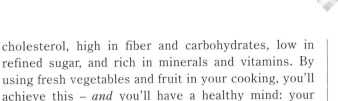

cholesterol, high in fiber and carbohydrates, low in refined sugar, and rich in minerals and vitamins. By using fresh vegetables and fruit in your cooking, you'll achieve this – *and* you'll have a healthy mind: your conscience is clear because nothing died for you today.

Q I want to lose weight. Is it possible to diet in a healthy vegetarian way?

A Yes, and very enjoyably: by eating large amounts of fresh vegetables and fruit and cutting back on your dairy intake, you'll get all the nutrients you need – minus the calories. You'll have a high-fiber diet – so you won't feel as hungry – and you'll find it a very tasty way to lose weight.

Q What would happen to the animals if nobody ate them?

A They'd be a lot happier, for a start. It's certainly not true that we'd be over-run with animals. There are so many "food" animals on the planet because they are over-bred by humans. For instance, in a farmyard a sow will produce about six piglets a year, but intensive farming has interfered with her to the extent that she can now produce 20 piglets a year. That's not natural.

Pigs, cows, and sheep are not going to become extinct if people stop eating them. To my knowledge, no species of animal has died out simply because humans stopped killing it.

Nature balances her own – she doesn't need us to interfere.

Q How many people are vegetarian?

A In six words – millions and more by the minute.

Few people in the West stop to think that vegetarianism is a way of life for vast numbers of people – all the tens of millions of Hindus and Buddhists for a start. There have been vegetarians on this planet since human life began – in fact the recent discovery of the oldest human fossil, in East Africa in 1994, indicates that Early Man (*Homo rudolfiensis*) was strictly vegetarian. Examination of the contents of his stomach revealed he lived entirely on a diet of grains, nuts, and vegetables.

As far back as the 6th Century B.C., Pythagoras was advocating vegetarianism, and many of the greatest thinkers since have been vegetarians, as were Plotinus, Plutarch, Diogenes, and Ovid. So, too, was Buddha. In

fact, it is interesting to note that many of the great minds that have shaped civilization belonged to vegetarians – people like Luther, Alexander Pope, Shelley, Thoreau, Gandhi, Milton, Da Vinci, Voltaire, Wordsworth, Tolstoy, Blake, and Benjamin Franklin. And people like George Bernard Shaw, who said: "While we ourselves are the living graves of murdered beasts, how can we expect any ideal conditions on this earth?"

Now, many people in the U.K. and U.S.A. are heeding Shaw's wisdom. In the U.K., seven percent of the population are declared veggies. More than 10 percent of British students are vegetarian, and the numbers are growing daily, especially among young girls – in one recent survey of teenage schoolgirls, 57 percent of those aged under 14 said they were vegetarian. In the U.S.A. the number of vegetarians has almost *doubled* over the past ten years from 6.5 million to 12.4 million.

Also, a recent official report by the British Frozen Food Information Service on hot-food trends in the 21st Century estimated that during the next decade as many as 20 percent of the people in Britain may become vegetarian.

So there are quite a few of us.

Q Is it safe to bring up children on a meatless diet?

A Totally safe. I looked into this with a nutritionist when we first went veggie, and provided that your children are fed a balanced diet with enough protein, minerals, and vitamins – preferably from fresh vegetables and fruit – and in the case of younger children some fat for energy, they can be vegetarians from birth.

Q Are desserts always vegetarian?

A No, check the labels for gelatin, the base of most fruit jellos, and for rennet and whey. Processed desserts may contain some emulsifiers (see What should I look for on labels?, below). Safest of all, make your own desserts – they'll probably be tastier.

Q What do I say to my friends?

A You could try saying what I do when I cook them a meal: "Try this, you'll love it." There is no reason for any vegetarian to feel apologetic about what he or she chooses to eat. Personally, I think the reasons I've listed

above are more than good enough reasons not to eat animals, but if you feel peer pressure, maybe you could say what one of my daughters said when she was asked how she felt about not eating meat. She said, "I feel like I have a clear conscience."

Q How will I fit in with family meals?

A You'll fit in fine, because vegetarian cooking is so simple. If the family meal consists of the traditional meat and two veg, then just leave the meat off your plate and fill the gap with either a cheese or egg dish or any of the meatless meals such as veggie sausages, burgers, pies, and pastas that are available today.

But once you get into this new way of eating I bet you'll find that the meals are so tasty and healthy that before long other members of your family will want to try them, too.

Q What about eating out in restaurants or entertaining friends?

A You'll have a good choice these days. Italian, Chinese, Indian, and Mexican restaurants are ideal because many of their traditional dishes are meatless anyway. Even French restaurants usually have mushroom, rice, or egg dishes to choose from.

As for eating with friends – if you're cooking, be proud to be veggie and be adventurous. There are dishes in this book to suit every appetite. Don't feel you'll be alienating your friends because, while many people do eat meat, I don't know of any who *only* eat meat. So, seeing vegetables on their plate is hardly going to be alien to them.

The other trick is not to tell them. With the abundance of meatless meals on the market, you can quite easily cook a meal that looks and tastes like meat.

Q Where do I buy meatless products?

A Although it used to be only health-food stores that stocked meatless meals, you'll find them widely available in any good supermarket chain now. If your supermarket doesn't stock them, ask them to.

Q What's the difference between free-range eggs and other eggs?

A Free-range hens are just that – they can roam indoors or outdoors, they live as near to their natural state as possible, and they have a balanced diet. They are not overcrowded and they are healthy.

Barn chickens are kept indoors in so-called barns without much daylight and in more crowded conditions than their free-ranging cousins.

Factory or battery hens are, in my opinion and in the opinion of most vegetarians, treated with great cruelty. They are cooped up in tiny spaces, frequently spending their entire lives in a wire cage. They are packed together, away from sunlight, and they often suffer deformities of the feet as they cannot move far and are forced to stand on wire netting. They are debeaked at birth to prevent them attacking each other in their madness. They are doped with large doses of antibiotics to prevent disease spreading in their overcrowded conditions, and their lives are basically miserable. The picture of misery is made clear by an analogy provided by the British Royal Society for the Prevention of Cruelty to Animals, which said that the space allocated to a hen in a battery hen house is the equivalent to stuffing a budgerigar into a jam jar.

Q Why should I eat organic products?

A I believe our food should be as natural as it is possible to grow it. I don't wish to eat fruit and vegetables that have been "bettered" with chemicals and pesticides – simply because I do not want, nor do I need, to have pesticides in my diet. I know that some fruit and vegetables are treated with substances to give them a longer shelf life or to make them look more attractive, but I'd rather have my food grown by Mother Nature than by the chemical industry.

Unfortunately there is currently little demand for organic produce. It is not always easily available, prices are quite high, and people have become accustomed to large and perfectly formed vegetables. However, it is up to the individual to create a greater demand, which will eventually bring about a reduction in cost.

Q What should I look for on labels to avoid animal products?

A It is surprising how many animal derivatives are contained in everyday products – your soap could contain lard, your cookies and crackers animal fats – which is why it is important to check *all* labels.

Beware gelatin, the gelling agent found in many foods, which is produced from animal bones and hooves.

Watch out for whey, the liquid part of milk that remains after the separation of the curds by rennet – usually animal – during the cheese-making process.

If you need to take vitamins, make sure that the capsules are not made from gelatine and check that none of the ingredients is an animal derivative. In particular, avoid added vitamin D, which is often animal-derived. Vitamin D3 is taken from lanolin, from sheep's wool, but not necessarily from live sheep.

Watch out for emulsifiers – some are derived from animal fats.

Even your household products contain animal derivatives, so check these carefully. Finally, your beauty products may contain collagen and glycerine, and these may be animal derivatives too.

Q Are meatless meals time-consuming to prepare?

A No, just the opposite. They are quick and simple to cook because vegetables require so much less cooking time than meat.

Q What can I feed to my dog?

A There are several brands of dried vegetarian dog food available, all carefully prepared to give a nutritional balance. The brand I am associated with is called Best. My dogs love it and I've had lots of letters from people telling me that Best has helped with their dog's stomach problems and skin conditions. Vets recommend it.

You can also give your pets wholesome bits of home cooking, but don't give them spicy foods because these may upset their stomachs, and avoid sugary foods as these will make them fat. Give dogs a piece of carrot or apple to chew on instead of a bone.

Q Isn't meatless food boring?

A Not if you like good, healthy, tasty, and colorful food. Because of what we *don't* eat, vegetarianism is about *life* – saving it and enjoying it. That shouldn't be boring. Anyway, try any recipe in this book and see for yourself.

Q What foods shall I keep in store and how do I prepare them?

A Read the following pages!

The Vegetarian Pantry

Basic Processed Foods

- canned tomatoes
- canned whole-kernel corn
- canned beans: lima, cannellini, red kidney, borlotti, pinto, etc.
- canned baked beans
- pasta: whole-wheat and plain
- whole-wheat bread
- soy products: soy milk, tofu, tempeh, vegetarian mince, vegetarian steak chunks, soy sauce, tamari
- vegetable bouillon cubes
- vegetarian gravy mix
- Marmite, yeast extract
- curry powder
- tomato paste
- tomato ketchup, pickles, relishes, chutneys, mustards
- mayonnaise
- Asian sauces: black bean, garlic, yellow bean, etc
- Mexican taco sauces and relishes

Frozen Products

- there is now a wide range of readymade frozen vegetarian meals available from supermarkets, including my own brand. These convenient products are ideal for busy cooks

Dairy Products

- free-range eggs
- vegetarian cheese
- plain yogurt

Spreads, Oils and Vinegars

- no-cholesterol margarine (read the label for hidden animal products)
- tahini
- vegetable pastes
- vinegars: cider, wine, rice, balsamic
- olive oil
- vegetable oils: sunflower, grapeseed, soy, peanut
- sesame oil
- walnut oil
- honey, jams (low sugar and homemade), maple syrup, corn syrup

Cereals

- barley, buckwheat, cornmeal, millet, oats, wheat
- rice
- wild rice
- unbleached organic flour

Dried Fruit

- raisins, golden raisins, currants
- apples
- apricots
- candied cherries
- candied mixed peel
- peaches
- pears
- prunes

Dried Legumes

- dried beans: black, soy, borlotti, navy, Great Northern, mung, red kidney, black-eyed peas
- lentils: red, green, brown
- split peas
- chick peas (garbanzos)

Basic Plant Foods

- seeds: pumpkin, sesame, sunflower, poppy
- nuts: almonds, brazils, cashews, hazelnuts, peanuts, pecans, pine nuts, pistachios, walnuts
- dried/flaked coconut
- capers
- olives
- sun-dried tomatoes
- chiles: dried and in brine

Herbs and Spices

- sea salt, peppercorns
- vanilla: beans, extract
- herbal teas
- the complete range: fresh and dried herbs, whole and ground spices, to your taste

Fruit and Vegetables

- plenty of fresh, organic fruits and vegetables in season

Legumes

Legumes, which include beans, peas and lentils, are very versatile, and they are an excellent source of protein, carbohydrate, vitamins and minerals, as well as being low in fat and high in fiber. The soy bean is the best source of quality protein.

Dried legumes need to be soaked overnight, in plenty of water to cover, before cooking. The exceptions are lentils and split peas: large whole lentils and large split peas need only 2–3 hours soaking, and very small red lentils and small split peas need no soaking at all.

To cook legumes, drain off the soaking water and rinse them, then put into a saucepan and cover with fresh water. (If cooking red kidney beans, bring to a boil, boil for 10 minutes, then drain and put back in the pan with fresh cold water to cover.) Add a bay leaf and a slice or two of onion for extra flavor. Bring to a boil and simmer, covered, for the time given in the chart below. Wait to add salt until 10 minutes before the end of the cooking time – it toughens the skins and hardens them if you add it earlier.

Dried legumes double their weight after being soaked and cooked, so when using them instead of canned legumes in a recipe, use half the weight of the canned legumes given. In other words, for 8 ounces canned kidney beans, soak and cook 4 ounces dried kidney beans.

When using canned legumes in a recipe, it's best to add them towards the end of the cooking time so that they don't go mushy. Drain them well and rinse under running cold water before you use them.

COOKING TIMES FOR LEGUMES, AFTER SOAKING

Aduki beans . . . . 30–60 minutes
Black beans . . . . 1½ hours
Borlotti beans . . . . 1 hour
Lima or butter beans . . . . 1–1½ hours
Cannellini beans . . . . 1 hour
Chick peas . . . . 1½–2 hours
Flageolets . . . . 45 minutes
Lentils, large brown or green . . . . 45 minutes
Mung beans . . . . 40 minutes
Navy beans . . . . 1–1½ hours
Red kidney beans . . . . 1–1½ hours
Soy beans . . . . 3–4 hours
Split peas, large . . . . 40–50 minutes

COOKING TIMES FOR LEGUMES WHICH REQUIRE
NO PRE-SOAKING

Lentils, small red . . . . 20–30 minutes
Split peas, small . . . . 45–60 minutes

Soy Products

The soy bean is the seed of the soy bean plant. It has been used as a staple in the Chinese diet for more than 4,000 years. From the soy bean come many soy products that are widely used in a vegetarian diet. These include:
• soy milk, which is made by soaking soy beans in water and then straining. Soy cheese and soy yogurt are made from soy milk.
• tofu, which is a curd made from coagulated soy milk. (Vegans can use tofu in place of yogurt in soups, dips, salad dressings, and sauces. "Silken" tofu, which is widely available, is light and creamy and works very well in all these recipes.)
• tempeh, which is a fermented soy bean paste made by mixing cooked soy beans with a fungus that holds it together.
• miso, which is a fermented condiment made from soy beans, grain (rice or barley), salt, and water.
• soy sauce (shoyu), which is made by fermenting soy beans with cracked roasted wheat, salt, and water.
• tamari, which is another soy sauce, similar to shoyu but slightly stronger and made without wheat.
• soy margarine and soy oil, both of which are high in polyunsaturated fats and low in saturated fats.

• soy flour.

• TVP, or textured vegetable protein, which is de-fatted soy flour, processed and dried to provide a substance that has a spongy texture, similar to meat. A good source of fiber and high quality protein, TVP is also fortified with vitamin B12.

Wheat

Wheat protein, which is derived from wheat gluten, can be processed to resemble closely the texture of meat and is widely used as a meat substitute.

Cooking with Meat Substitutes

Meat substitutes are available ground as mince and cubed as chunks, as well as in the form of sausages and burgers. All can be found in supermarkets and health food stores. The joy of using vegetarian mince and chunks is that you can take them straight from the freezer – there's no need to thaw them. Just measure out the amount called for in the recipe and add it as directed. You can use it in curries, chili non carne (see page 55), in a shepherd's pie (page 101) or a bolognese sauce (page 154) for spaghetti or lasagne – any dish where you would expect to find mince or stew beef.

To brown vegetarian mince or steak chunks (which brings out their flavor), sauté them lightly in 2 tbsp hot oil for each ½ pound. If you are in a hurry you can use these products without browning them first, although they will be slightly less tasty.

As a general rule, every pound of mince or chunks needs at least 2 cups of liquid in the sauce since they are usually more absorbent than meat. Neither vegetarian mince nor chunks need much salt, so season judiciously.

Vegetarian Cheese

To make cheese, a substance called rennet is used to coagulate milk, separating it into curds and whey. The curds are treated to make cheese, and the liquid whey finds its way into margarines and many other products. Vegetarian cheese is made with rennets of non-animal origin.

Fig leaves, thistle, melon and safflower have provided the country housewife with plant rennets in the past, but today most vegetarian cheeses are made using rennet produced by a fungus, *Mucor miehei*, or from a bacteria (*Bacillus subtilis*). Animal rennet, which contains the enzyme chymosin, is usually obtained from the stomach of newly born calves. Advances in genetic engineering have led to the synthesizing of chymosin, which may soon replace animal rennet.

Vegetarian cheeses are usually clearly labeled. Vegetarian versions of cream cheese and other soft cheeses, cheddar, cheshire, double gloucester, stilton, brie, dolcelatte and other blue cheeses, feta and ricotta, can often be found in major supermarkets. Cottage cheese is always vegetarian. Parmesan is normally made with animal rennet, although a vegetarian version is emerging. Mozzarella is not always vegetarian.

Cheese is a good source of protein, as well as calcium, zinc, vitamin B12 and a little iron. New vegetarians should be wary of eating too much cheese as it contains a lot of saturated fat and can lead to high cholesterol levels.

Mushrooms

In some parts of the world gathering wild mushrooms is a national pastime, a family outing to harvest the cèpes, chanterelles, boletus, parasol, and field mushrooms that grow in the woods and fields at certain times of the year. Gathering mushrooms is a wonderful experience, akin to a treasure hunt, and you are well rewarded when you deliver them to the table.

Obviously you have to be careful not to pick the wrong ones, but the poisonous mushrooms are easily identifiable with a good field guide. So take to the woods and fields and enjoy the pleasures of both the hunt and the table.

Nutrition for Vegetarians

A good diet is a balanced diet: it is the overall mixture that counts. The important thing is to eat a wide variety of foods to give you the nutrients that the body needs to maintain growth, to repair itself, to provide energy, and to resist infection. At least once a day, everyone should eat a well-balanced meal, which means one that contains sufficient carbohydrate, protein, fat, dietary fiber, water, vitamins, and minerals for individual needs. These dietary needs vary according to sex, age, activity levels, physical condition, and climate. There are numerous books that give detailed information on this complex subject, but the guidelines here should help you ensure that you are getting a good nutritional balance in your daily diet.

Energy and Water

Food is the fuel that gives the human body energy, thus enabling it to work. The right amount of food is essential for normal biological processes such as breathing and pumping blood round the body, to perform muscular work and to maintain body temperature. Certain foods provide more energy than others; some provide it quickly while others release it slowly into the system.

Water comprises two-thirds of our body weight, and we cannot survive for more than a few days without water. Many foods contain high levels, but it is also important to drink sufficient water on a daily basis: experts suggest 1 to 2 quarts every day.

Protein

Proteins are made up from various combinations of amino acids that are required by our bodies for growth and repair. Both plant proteins and animal proteins contain these amino acids, so it is a fallacy that we can only get protein from an animal source. Excess amounts of protein cannot be stored in the body, so eating more than you need can have no benefit. In fact, it can be harmful – many western meat-eating diets contain far too much protein and this is now thought to cause diseases including certain cancers and osteoporosis, as well as poor kidney function.

A healthy, balanced diet containing a variety of foods will provide you with all the protein you require.

GOOD SOURCES OF PROTEIN Legumes (in particular soy beans), soy products (tofu, soy milk, etc), nuts, seeds, rice, pasta, wheat flour, bread, muesli, oatmeal, cheese, eggs, milk, yogurt, potatoes, peas, cauliflower, broccoli, garlic, corn.

Carbohydrate

Carbohydrate is a major source of energy in the diet, and most of it is provided by plant foods. There are three main types of carbohydrate in food: sugars, starches, and cellulose. Cellulose is the indigestible part of plant foods and is the main constituent of dietary fiber. This stimulates the digestive system, helps prevent constipation and reduces the risk of colon cancer and diverticular disease.

GOOD SOURCES OF CARBOHYDRATE Legumes, rice, pasta, buckwheat groats, bulgur wheat, oatmeal, bread, nuts, potatoes, root vegetables, peas, corn, onions, garlic, dried apricots, bananas, mangoes.

GOOD SOURCES OF DIETARY FIBER Legumes, nuts, whole-wheat bread, whole-wheat pasta, wheat bran, oats and other whole grains, most vegetables (particularly beans, cabbage, carrots, potatoes), raspberries, blackberries, redcurrants, dates, figs, prunes, dried apricots.

Fat and Cholesterol

Fat provides energy in a more concentrated form than carbohydrate and converts very easily into body fat. Although a certain amount of fat is necessary to provide warmth and essential nutrients and to protect the internal organs, the average western diet contains too much. Fats from animal sources contain a high proportion of saturated fatty acids, which raise blood cholesterol levels and increase the risk of heart disease.

Cholesterol is unique to animals and humans. It is made mainly in the liver and is present in all of the body's tissues. We need cholesterol but we do not necessarily need it in the diet: for some people an excess can cause health problems. This is why people on an animal-product-free diet are thought to be less at risk from heart disease.

SOURCES OF FAT Cheese, cream, yogurt, whole milk, butter, margarine, egg yolk, nuts, seeds, avocados, olives, vegetable oils, oats.

Vitamins

Small amounts of vitamins are essential for the regulation of all bodily processes. With the exception of vitamin D, the body cannot make its own vitamins, and some cannot be stored. Vitamins must therefore be obtained from food on a daily basis. A vegetarian diet can provide all the necessary vitamins.

VITAMIN A
Required for healthy skin and mucus membranes, and for night vision. Thought to help prevent the development of cancer.

GOOD SOURCES OF VITAMIN A Butter, margarine, milk, cheese, yogurt, cream, sweet potatoes, butternut squash, carrots, red sweet peppers, chile peppers, leeks, lettuce, broccoli, Swiss chard, spinach, tomatoes, watercress, basil, cilantro, parsley, apricots, canteloupe melons, mangoes, papayas, guavas, persimmons.

B VITAMINS
A group of eight actual vitamins and several vitamin-like compounds. The main ones include:
Thiamin (B1): Releases energy from carbohydrate, alcohol, and fat.
Riboflavin (B2): Releases energy from protein, fat, and carbohydrate.
Niacin (B3): Involved in the oxidative release of energy from food; protects the skin and helps improve circulation.
Vitamin B6: Essential for protein metabolism, and for the formation of hemoglobin – the pigment in the blood that carries oxygen round the body.
Vitamin B12: Helps protect nerves and is involved in the formation of red blood cells in the bone marrow.
Folate: Involved in the formation of new cells and therefore essential for the normal growth and development of the fetus.

GOOD SOURCES OF B VITAMINS Eggs, cheese, milk, legumes, whole-wheat bread, brown rice, fortified cereals, nuts, seeds, yeast extract, avocados, cauliflower, cabbage, peas, potatoes, mushrooms, green leafy vegetables, dates, figs, currants, dried apricots, clementines, canteloupe melon.

VITAMIN C
Essential for the formation of bones, teeth and tissues. Speeds the healing of wounds, helps maintain elasticity of the skin, aids the absorption of iron and improves resistance to infection. May help prevent the occurrence and development of cancer.

GOOD SOURCES OF VITAMIN C Broccoli, Brussels sprouts, cauliflower, cabbage, snow-peas, green leafy vegetables, red sweet peppers, chile peppers, watercress, parsley, black currants, strawberries, kiwi fruit, guavas, citrus fruit.

NOTE: With the exception of niacin (B3), these vitamins are easily destroyed by heat. Vitamin C is easily destroyed by exposure to air, and all are unstable in alkaline conditions and are water-soluble. So to maximize the intake of these vitamins, food sources should be prepared, cooked, and served quickly. For example, steaming vegetables reduces the amount of time they are exposed to heat and minimizes vitamin loss in the cooking water.

VITAMIN D
Needed for the absorption of calcium and the regulation of calcium levels in the blood. Sunlight activates the metabolism of vitamin D in the body.

GOOD SOURCES OF VITAMIN D Butter, margarine, cheese, cream, yogurt, milk, eggs, sunlight.

VITAMIN E
An anti-oxidant that protects the cells from attack by reactive forms of oxygen and free radicals. Involved in red blood cell formation.

GOOD SOURCES OF VITAMIN E Vegetable oils, nuts and nut oils, seeds, egg yolk, margarine, Parmesan, cheddar, chick peas, soy beans (and soy products such as TVP, tofu and soy milk), wheat germ, oatmeal, avocados, olives, carrots, parsnips, red sweet peppers, green leafy vegetables, sweet potatoes, tomatoes, corn, watercress.

VITAMIN K
Needed for effective blood clotting. A deficiency is rare due to bacterial synthesis within the body. Vitamin K is found in most vegetables.

Minerals

Minerals perform a variety of important functions in the human body. A balanced intake is important for long-term good health. Excess of any mineral can be as dangerous as too little.

CALCIUM

Calcium is the most abundant mineral in the body, and is needed for building strong bones and teeth, for muscle contraction and blood clotting. Healthy bones are not only reliant on a good calcium intake but on regular exercise and vitamin D, which aids calcium absorption.

It should also be noted, however, that too much calcium can also be harmful as the excess is deposited in internal organs such as kidneys. This can cause serious problems and even be fatal.

Dairy foods have traditionally been thought of as the principal source of calcium, but have you ever stopped to think where the cow gets its calcium from – certainly not from dairy products!

GOOD SOURCES OF CALCIUM Milk, cheese, yogurt, raw sesame seeds, tofu, bread, nuts, legumes, okra, broccoli, watercress, onions, green leafy vegetables, sea vegetables, dried fruit such as raisins, apricots, pears and peaches, rhubarb, lemons, oranges, hard water.

MAGNESIUM

Needed for strong bones, and for the functioning of some of the enzymes involved in energy utilization.

GOOD SOURCES OF MAGNESIUM Cream, yogurt, cheese, eggs, bread, papadums, wheat bran, bulgur wheat, oatmeal, soy flour, whole-wheat flour, brown rice, whole-wheat pasta, nuts, seeds, legumes, green leafy vegetables, sea vegetables, dried fruit such as apricots, pears and peaches.

IRON

Essential component of hemoglobin, the red pigment in blood which transports oxygen though the body. Iron also assists in the production of red blood corpuscles, the metabolism of B vitamins and the functioning of several enzymes. Iron deficiency, which causes anemia, is the most prevalent nutritional problem worldwide. It has been shown that vegetarians are no more likely to suffer from it than non-vegetarians. A good intake of vitamin C enhances absorption of iron.

GOOD SOURCES OF IRON Eggs, legumes, whole-wheat bread, wheat bran, papadums, cashew nuts, pine nuts, pumpkin seeds, cumin seeds, sesame seeds, green leafy vegetables, watercress, sea vegetables, basil, mint, parsley, black currants, dried fruits such as raisins, prunes, figs, and peaches, cocoa.

ZINC

Present in every part of the body and vital for the healthy working of many of its functions, including a major role in enzyme reactions, the immune system and resistance to infection. It plays a crucial role in growth and cell division, in insulin activity and liver function. Men need more zinc than women because semen contains 100 times more zinc than is found in the blood, and so the more sexually active a man is, the more zinc he will require.

GOOD SOURCES OF ZINC Cheese, egg yolk, legumes, whole-wheat bread, wheat bran, soy flour, yeast, nuts, pumpkin seeds, sesame seeds, tahini paste, green vegetables, garlic.

POTASSIUM

Important in maintaining the body's correct balance of fluids, required for nerve and muscle function, and the metabolism of sugar and protein.

GOOD SOURCES OF POTASSIUM Yogurt, legumes, soy flour, nuts, seeds, green vegetables, potatoes, beets, chile peppers, garlic, sea vegetables, rhubarb, bananas, dates, dried apricots, prunes.

Bibliography

Beyond Beef, *Jeremy Rifkin (Penguin)* • Diet for a New America, *John Robbins (Stillpoint)* • Why You Don't Need Meat, *Peter Cox (Thorsons)* • Fit for Life, *Harvey and Marilyn Diamond (Bantam)* • Diet for a Small Planet, *Frances Moore Lappé (Ballantine)* • Agricultural Statistics 1989, *United States Department of Agriculture, Washington DC* • State of the World's Children, *UNICEF* • The Worldwatch Institute, *cited by Boyce Rensberger, New York Times (25 October 1974)* • Soil and Water, *"Water Requirements for Food Production", Tom Aldridge and Herb Schlubach, Fall 1978, no. 38, University of California Cooperative Extension* • Journal of the American Medical Association, *"Premature Mortality from Coronary Heart Disease: The Gramingham Study", T. Gordon* • American Journal of Clinical Nutrition, *"Nutritional Studies of Vegetarians IV: Dietary Acids and Serum Cholesterol Levels", M. Hardinge* • Revista de Biologgia Tropical, *"Forest to Pasture: Development or Destruction?", James Parsons, Vol. 24 (supp. I), 1976* • The British Medical Journal, *"Risk of Death from Cancer and Ischaemic Heart Disease in Meat and Non-meat Eaters", Vol. 308, pp 1667-74* • Diet, Nutrition and the Prevention of Chronic Diseases, *The World Health Organisation Study Group*

Index

Index